EXPLANATION

of

The Book of Revelation

†

Explanation of

THE BOOK OF
REVELATION

By C. H. LITTLE

CONCORDIA PUBLISHING HOUSE
SAINT LOUIS, MISSOURI

FOREWORD

Of all the writings in the New Testament the Book of Revelation is the hardest to understand. Heretical views of various types have been drawn from it by church bodies and by numerous sects in Christendom. It is a unique book, being the only book in the New Testament that is of a strictly prophetical nature. It is further unique in this, that prophecy here takes the special form of an apocalypse, wherein the future is unveiled in the form of pictures, or visions. It also contains more figurative expressions than any other book of the Bible. The great fault of the interpretation of the Book of Revelation has been, and still is, to take figurative language literally; and this has led to manifold errors and even to contradiction of other plain passages of Scripture. For this reason I have deemed it advisable to put forth in this little volume a clear and popular exposition of this wonderful book in accordance with its style and context in order that the reader may understand its actual teaching. In referring to the text the Authorized Version will generally be followed, with only one exception, namely, the frequently occurring mistranslation "four beasts," which in the Revised Version is rendered "four living creatures," but which should more accurately read: "four living ones."

Another matter about which there has been difference of opinion is the question: By whom was the Book of Revelation written? In answer to this it may be said: While in it the writer styles himself simply John and claims for himself no other distinction than that he is a servant of the Lord Jesus Christ, many things in the book tend to show that he is no other than the Apostle John. He distinctly asserts that the revelation which he here records was received by him directly from the Lord Jesus while he was an exile "for the Word of God and for the testimony of Jesus Christ" on the Isle of Patmos (cf. 1:2, 9). Antiquity unanimously connected such

exile with the life of the Apostle John. The letters of Jesus
in Chapters 2 and 3 were addressed to the seven churches
of Asia Minor. This was the special sphere of activity of
the Apostle John after 67 A. D. The external evidence for
the Apostle John's authorship is also quite strong. Justin
Martyr, Irenaeus, Tertullian, the Canon of Muratori, Origen,
and Hippolytus all bear strongly convincing testimony to
the Johannean authorship. To the objection raised by some
critics that there is a manifest difference in style and language
in this book from John's other writings, it may be replied that
this is accounted for by the fact that prophetic discourse calls
for a different form of presentation from that of historical
narrative.

While the Book of Revelation was written to the seven
churches of Asia Minor to meet their immediate needs, it must
not be regarded as confined to them; but, like all the New
Testament Epistles, it addresses messages of comfort and
consolation to the children of God in all their trials and tribulations unto the end of time.

Revelation may be divided as follows:

Introduction (Chapter 1:1-8).

I. The Seven Epistles to the Churches in Asia Minor
(Chapters 1:9 to 3:22).

II. Revelation Concerning the Consummation of God's
Kingdom (Chapters 4 to 22).

Methods of Interpretation. — Three methods of interpret-
ing the prophecies in Revelation have been proposed. The
first of these regards the prophecies as already fulfilled in
the past. The second regards them as attaining fulfillment
only at the end of the world, in close connection with Christ's
second advent. The third looks upon the prophecies as being
progressively fulfilled during the history of the present dispensation. This last method is the one adopted by the vast
majority of Protestant commentators. This, as adhering most
closely to the text, is the only proper method of interpretation.

C. H. LITTLE

CONTENTS

The

BOOK

of

REVELATION

✝

INTRODUCTION

Chapter 1:1-8

1. *The revelation of Jesus Christ which God gave unto Him, to show unto His servants things which must shortly come to pass; and He sent and signified it by His angel unto His servant John;* 2. *who bare record of the Word of God and of the testimony of Jesus Christ and of all things that he saw.* 3. *Blessed is he that readeth, and they that hear the words of this prophecy and keep those things which are written therein; for the time is at hand.* 4. *John to the seven churches which are in Asia: Grace be unto you, and peace, from Him which is and which was and which is to come; and from the seven Spirits which are before His throne,* 5. *and from Jesus Christ, who is the faithful Witness and the First-Begotten of the dead and the Prince of the kings of the earth. Unto Him that loved us and washed us from our sins in His own blood* 6. *and hath made us kings and priests unto God and His Father: to Him be glory and dominion forever and ever. Amen.* 7. *Behold, He cometh with clouds; and every eye shall see Him, and they also which pierced Him: and all kindreds of the earth shall wail because of Him. Even so, Amen.* 8. *I am Alpha and Omega, the Beginning and the Ending, saith the Lord, which is and which was and which is to come, the Almighty.*

In verses 1-3 the prophetic character and chief contents of this book are indicated, and a high commendation of it to every Christian is given. The very first word, Revelation, literally, Apocalypse, gives the name to the book and at the same time indicates its pur-

pose or character. It is a revelation, i. e., an unveiling of
hidden things, or in other words, of divine mysteries. And
the words that immediately follow in this first verse show
that this revelation was made by Jesus Christ, the great
Revealer of the Godhead; and that He made this revelation not independently, but only as it had been given to
Him by God the Father. This is in thorough accord with
many passages of the Fourth Gospel (cf. John 5:36;
12:49-50; 14:11; and other passages). The purpose of
this revelation which God gave to His only-begotten Son
was to show certain things to the servants of Jesus Christ,
i. e., to believing Christians. What these things were
is indicated in the words: "things which must shortly
come to pass," i. e., things which according to the will
and knowledge of God are bound to occur. The word
"shortly" here is not, however, to be understood as referring to immediate fulfillment, since John himself
clearly distinguishes the beginning of final completion
from the completion itself (cf. 1:9; 13:10; 14:12). Of this
revelation of future things, open and known to God, but
veiled to the eyes of men, it is declared that the Lord sent
it by one of His angels, who are His ministering spirits
and delight to do His will. It is further asserted that He
signified it, i. e., revealed it to His servant John. This occurred in visions and pictures, as the contents show,
which are to some extent explained. This message, which
consisted "of the Word of God and of the testimony of
Jesus Christ and of all things that he [John] saw," John
did not keep to himself, but was an instrument in God's
hands in spreading it far and wide. In v. 3 we have the
first of the seven beatitudes in the Book of Revelation.
This beatitude is properly placed at the head of them all.
It not only commends the book to believers, but assures
every believer who reads it that he will find in it a source
of blessedness, a means of participation in the Kingdom

of Glory. But since in this early age of the Christian era many Christians were not able to read, this blessedness is not restricted to readers only, but includes also those who hear the words of this prophecy. Both the readers and the hearers who, in steadfast faith, carefully observe the injunctions here recorded and rely upon the precious promises of the prophecy are pronounced blessed. The reason for this beatitude is clearly stated in the concluding words: "for the time is at hand." This expression refers to a definite, fixed time – the time appointed of God for bringing blessedness to the faithful. This brings at once to our mind the words of St. Paul: "Behold, now is the accepted time; behold, now is the day of salvation" (2 Cor. 6:2). The intimation here is that we Christians are living in the last days of God's dispensation for the world. This serves as a reminder to us that the age in which we live is no time for slumbering or slothfulness, but for vigilance. And this accords with the Lord's own frequent admonitions in the Gospels, such as Matt. 25:13: "Watch therefore, for ye know neither the day nor the hour wherein the Son of Man cometh."

The remaining verses (4-8) of the Introduction set forth the dedication of this book to the seven churches of Asia and constitute the very heart of the message which this precious book proclaims. The first word that John uses here is "grace" – the free grace, or unmerited favor, of God which the sinner receives in the glorious Gospel of salvation, the glad tidings of redemption through the love of God the Father, our Creator, of God the Son, our Redeemer, and of God the Holy Ghost, our Sanctifier. This first word is followed by the word "peace," which is the effect of divine grace and follows immediately upon the reconciliation of the sinner with God (cf. Rom. 5:1; Phil. 4:7). This grace, with the peace which inevitably follows, comes from God, who is de-

scribed here, as nowhere else in the New Testament outside of Revelation, as "which is and which was and which
is to come." By this characterization of God the author
stresses the immutability and eternity of God and His
almighty power in ruling over the destinies of men and
of the hostile world, and in bringing all things under
His impending judgment. To this is added a peculiar
designation of the Holy Ghost, which likewise is employed nowhere else in Scripture outside of Revelation,
viz., "the seven Spirits which are before His throne."
The Spirit thus described is the Holy Spirit, the Spirit
who speaks to the churches (2:7; 3:28), the Spirit of God
(3:1; 5:6), and the Spirit who makes men prophets
(19:10). The number seven here is a concrete presentation indicating God's dealings with the world and has no
bearing on the sevenfold gifts of the Spirit referred to in
Is. 11:2. In the next verse St. John speaks of Jesus Christ,
placing Him on the same level with the Father and the
Spirit, thus completing the Trinitarian formula and declaring the Triune God, Father, Spirit, and Son, to be
the sole source of all grace and peace to which every
believing Christian falls heir. In the words that immediately follow he proceeds to describe Jesus in the most
glowing terms as "the faithful Witness and the First-
Begotten of the dead" and pictures Him in His exalted
glory at the right hand of divine majesty and power as
the Conqueror of death (cf. Col. 1:18) and Ruler over the
kings of the earth, ruling over all things in heaven and on
earth, or as he elsewhere expresses it, "Lord of Lords and
King of Kings" (cf. 17:14; 19:16). To this description,
the Apostle whom Jesus loved adds a fervent doxology to
the exalted Christ, in which he gives expression to Christ's
attitude toward His believing people from the beginning
to the end and to His unchanging and continuous love
for them. Our sins are here pictured as a binding chain

from which Christ has loosed us by means of His blood,
which He shed as a ransom for our sins. In v. 6, which
stands in close connection with this verse, John vividly
states the blessings which we as believers have as a result
of Christ's sacrificial and atoning death on our behalf and
as our Substitute. As a consequence of this we are in the
glorious situation of being a kingdom and priests unto
God and His Father. Let it be further noted that this
kingdom is no ordinary kingdom, but a spiritual kingdom,
in which all who have appropriated by faith the redemption wrought out for them by God's only-begotten Son,
Jesus Christ, have full and free access to the Throne of
Grace and can boldly present their petitions before God
with the full assurance that they will receive seasonable
help (Heb. 4:16). What a strong confirmation we have
here of the spiritual priesthood of all believers! And how
comforting this is! No wonder there follows immediately
as a fitting close to the statement just made: "to Him be
glory and dominion forever and ever. Amen." In v. 7 the
Apostle resumes the thought interrupted by the doxology
in the preceding verse. And that what he has to say is
of more than ordinary importance is indicated by the
interjection "Behold." And what he here depicts is nothing less than the second coming of Christ — a matter
which should be of intense interest and expectation to
every true believer. The description which is here given
of Christ's coming with clouds indicates both His majesty
and His coming as a coming for judgment (cf. Matt.
26:64). In the remainder of the verse Christ's coming is
depicted as a public coming, visible to all men and hidden
from none. This also is in strict accord with Christ's own
words in the Gospels concerning His second advent. The
words in v. 7 "and they also which pierced Him" are
explanatory of the preceding clause and clearly point out
that all the ungodly men upon earth, to whom by reason

of their unbelief, this sin is imputed, will behold Him as He comes in majesty, might, and glory to administer the final Judgment. The effect that His coming will have upon them is graphically described in the words: "and all kindreds [literally, 'tribes'] of the earth shall wail because of Him." The intimation here is that the time for repentance has passed, and only weeping and howling in helpless terror remains for them. This is surely a vivid description of the utter dejection and hopeless remorse of all unbelievers, as their never-ending horrible fate stares them in the face. That this is God's inexorable judgment upon them is confirmed by the solemn words "Even so, Amen."

In the next verse (v. 8) the Lord Himself is introduced as speaking. Herein proclaiming Himself as "Alpha and Omega, the Beginning and the Ending," Jesus asserts Himself to be true God from all eternity, as Lord God in the fullest sense of the term without any qualifications whatever. And by the words that follow: "which is and which was and which is to come," He eliminates all conception of time as applying to Himself and powerfully emphasizes the eternity of His existence. And this He climaxes with the attributive name "the Almighty," thus proclaiming as strongly as could possibly be done His absolute equality with the Father. Surely a firmer foundation could not be laid for our faith in Jesus Christ our Lord, whose name is the only "name under heaven given among men whereby we must be saved."

Part One
THE SEVEN EPISTLES TO THE
CHURCHES IN ASIA MINOR

CHAPTERS 1:9 TO 3:22

✝

9. *I, John, who also am your brother and companion in tribulation and in the kingdom and patience of Jesus Christ, was in the isle that is called Patmos, for the Word of God and for the testimony of Jesus Christ. 10. I was in the spirit on the Lord's day and heard behind me a great voice, as of a trumpet, 11. saying: I am Alpha and Omega, the First and the Last; and: What thou seest, write in a book, and send it unto the seven churches which are in Asia; unto Ephesus, and unto Smyrna, and unto Pergamos, and unto Thyatira, and unto Sardis, and unto Philadelphia, and unto Laodicea.*

In these verses John sets forth his commission to write. This is done in the very beginning in order that the entire book may be acknowledged to be that which it claims for itself in v. 1, "the revelation of Jesus Christ." In the opening words, "I John," we find a combination occurring only once again in the New Testament (Gal. 5:2, "I Paul"), but similar to many passages in the book of Daniel in the Old Testament. In addressing his fellow believers in this verse, he shows his close attachment to them, designating himself as their brother and as sharing with them in the tribulation which is theirs as servants of Jesus Christ in a hostile world and as having fellowship with them in the kingdom and patience of their gracious Lord, which is the common experience of all

those who endure tribulation for His sake. He now tells
them that he was on the isle of Patmos when he received
the revelation which he here records. This is in full accord
with tradition, which declares that he was banished to
this island by the decree of the Emperor of Rome. This
banishment, he assures his readers, was not for any crime
that he had committed or for any wrong that he had
done, but solely for his proclamation of the Word of God
and for his testimony to Jesus Christ, whom he so faithfully confessed. This gives the setting in which John
found himself when he received the revelations that now
follow. In vv. 10-11 he describes his situation in detail
and the motive which induced him to write this book.
Here, first of all, he declares that he was "in the spirit on
the Lord's day," i. e., in ecstasy, or a state of mind free
from distraction and suitable for the reception of a special divine revelation. The time when this occurred is
definitely stated as "on the Lord's day," namely, Sunday,
the day which commemorated the Lord's triumphal resurrection — a day which was set aside from the very beginning as the most suitable day for Christian worship.
Next he declares that, while he was in this state of
ecstasy, he heard a great sound like that of a trumpet,
a loud voice commissioning him as to what he should do.
The statement that he heard this voice from behind indicates that this divine utterance came to him as something surprising and unexpected. In v. 11 is given the
content of the voice which John heard. The first requirement was that he should write in a book the things which
he sees, i. e., a description of the visions presented to his
view. This is inclusive of the whole revelation that follows. The second requirement is that John is directed
not only to write the book, but to send it to its destination,
namely, to the seven cities here named. These cities were
the seats of the principal congregations in which Chris-

tianity had taken root and become established in pro-consular Asia. As the experiences of these congregations are typical of the progress of Christianity through all succeeding ages, the revelation recorded in this book applies equally to all future Christian congregations to the end of time.

Chapter 1:12-20

12. *And I turned to see the voice that spake with me. And being turned, I saw seven golden candlesticks;* 13. *and in the midst of the seven candlesticks One like unto the Son of Man, clothed with a garment down to the foot and girt about the paps with a golden girdle.* 14. *His head and His hairs were white like wool, as white as snow, and His eyes were as a flame of fire,* 15. *and His feet like unto fine brass, as if they burned in a furnace, and His voice as the sound of many waters.* 16. *And He had in His right hand seven stars; and out of His mouth went a sharp two-edged sword; and His countenance was as the sun shineth in his strength.* 17. *And when I saw Him, I fell at His feet as dead. And He laid His right hand upon me, saying unto me: Fear not; I am the First and the Last;* 18. *I am He that liveth and was dead; and, behold, I am alive forevermore, amen, and have the keys of hell and of death.* 19. *Write the things which thou hast seen, and the things which are, and the things which shall be hereafter;* 20. *the mystery of the seven stars which thou sawest in My right hand, and the seven golden candlesticks. The seven stars are the angels of the seven churches: and the seven candlesticks which thou sawest are the seven churches.*

In these verses John records the impression made upon him by the voice which he had heard, and describes in a vivid way the vision that he had seen. In v. 12 he declares that upon hearing the voice he turned, i. e., turned around, or turned backward (see v. 10). His

purpose in so doing, as he tells us, was to see whose was
the voice that thus spake. This indicates that the important thing was the message conveyed, the word heard.
The beginning of the description of what John saw now
follows. What he first saw was seven golden candlesticks,
representing, as v. 20 shows, the seven congregations
mentioned in the preceding verse. In these congregations
the entire Church is reflected. The fact that these candlesticks are of gold intimates the preciousness and beauty
of the Church and of all that is connected with it. In
vv. 13-16 John presents in a striking way the climax of
this vision. It is none other than "the Son of Man," Jesus
Christ, who is depicted here as appearing in all His divine
majesty, brilliancy, and glory. His hair, "white like wool,
as white as snow," is symbolical of eternity and reminds
us of the striking prophecies of Isaiah and Daniel concerning the coming of the promised Messiah (cf. Is. 9:6;
Dan. 7:13). In the description of His eyes as "a flame of
fire," there is signified His omniscience and His burning
zeal against all that is unholy and impure. In the description of His feet as "like unto fine brass, as if they burned
in a furnace," it is indicated that His feet are strong for
the purpose of treading down His unholy enemies, and it
carries with it the idea that the Lord is a consuming fire
to the unbelievers. And the description of His voice as
"the sound of many waters" represents the surging, ir-
repressible force of His voice directed against the enemies
of Christ and His Church, overwhelming them and hin-
dering the accomplishment of their designs. In this
vision John sees Christ having in His right hand seven
stars, which are, as he explains in v. 20, the angels of the
seven churches. This signifies that these churches are
His property and that He holds and protects them by
His almighty power (cf. John 10:28). This fact is stated
here for the comfort and encouragement of true believers

everywhere and of all time. Besides this, John sees a
sharp two-edged sword proceeding out of Christ's mouth.
This pictures Christ as a terror to all His foes. The sword
is His Word (cf. Heb. 4:12), with which He is able to
subdue all adversaries, and is wielded against all His
enemies, whether secret or open. As these enemies are
also the enemies of His people, this statement should be
of great comfort to us Christians. To this the Apostle
adds: "and His countenance was as the sun shineth in his
strength." These words apply to the whole appearance
of Christ in this vision. It was of so brilliant a nature
that it could be compared only to the sun shining in all
the fullness of its splendor. Such appearance brings to
believers assurance of light and power from their Lord;
but fills all unbelievers with terror and dismay.

In v. 17 statement is made of the immediate effect
upon John of the glorious appearance of his Lord. In the
presence of the Lord in all His majesty and glory, John is
smitten with mortal terror, and he confesses that he fell
down at His feet as dead. This is only the natural effect
of the majestic appearance of the Lord upon sinful man.
But John's terror, he tells us, did not last long. The Lord
immediately showed Himself gracious and friendly toward His servant, laying His right hand upon him and
accompanying this friendly sign with words of exceedingly precious assurance. His first words here are: "Fear
not," words which John, together with his fellow disciples, had frequently heard from the Lord's gracious
lips after His resurrection. This He follows up with the
words: "I am the First and the Last," words which, as
we have seen in v. 8, proclaim His eternal existence and
His essential deity.

To this the Lord adds in v. 18 as a climax: "I am He
that liveth and was dead; and, behold, I am alive for
evermore, amen." In these words, Jesus proclaims Him-

self the Living One who as such can also give life (cf.
John 5:21, 26; 11:25-26), and at the same time attests
His mediatorial death for all mankind upon the Cross,
whereby He made atonement for the sins of the whole
world. And in the words that follow He equally emphatically attests His glorious resurrection. He died indeed;
but death could not hold Him. He triumphed over it
and arose alive to die no more. He here shows Himself
the Living One who lives to all eternity (cf. John 5:21).
And by the words: "and have the keys of death and of
hell," He reveals conclusively to His beloved Apostle that
He is Lord and Master of both these realms, able to con-
sign to them and to deliver from them. What a comfort
for all believers is this, that their Lord's power is un-
limited, both to open and to close these realms! In the
succeeding verse the Lord, who had appeared to John,
commissions him to write. Drawing conclusion from the
preceding verses (17-18), where Christ introduces Himself as the majestic Lord, He instructs John as to what
he is to write, namely, the vision which he has just seen,
and all things, present and future, including the contents
of all the visions vouchsafed to him.

V. 20, the final verse in this chapter, is explanatory of
the "mystery" of the seven stars and the seven candlesticks which John has just seen in the vision. The Lord
expressly states here that the seven stars are the angels
of the seven churches; and that the seven candlesticks are
the seven churches. Considerable controversy has arisen
here as to the actual meaning of the word "angels." The
simplest explanation is that the "angels" symbolize the
pastors of these churches. Besides this, it is practically
inconceivable that John should be commissioned to write
to or act as the messenger to such a superterrestrial being
as an angel, instructing him what to do in connection with
each of these churches.

I. EPISTLE TO THE CHURCH
IN EPHESUS

Chapter 2:1-7

---

1. *Unto the angel of the church of Ephesus write: These things saith He that holdeth the seven stars in His right hand, who walketh in the midst of the seven golden candlesticks: 2. I know thy works, and thy labor, and thy patience, and how thou canst not bear them which are evil; and thou hast tried them which say they are apostles and are not, and hast found them liars; 3. and hast borne, and hast patience, and for My name's sake hast labored, and hast not fainted. 4. Nevertheless I have somewhat against thee, because thou hast left thy first love. 5. Remember, therefore, from whence thou art fallen, and repent, and do the first works; or else I will come unto thee quickly and will remove thy candlestick out of his place, except thou repent. 6. But this thou hast, that thou hatest the deeds of the Nicolaitanes, which I also hate. 7. He that hath an ear, let him hear what the Spirit saith unto the churches: To him that overcometh will I give to eat of the tree of life, which is in the midst of the Paradise of God.*

"Unto the angel of the church of Ephesus write." These are the Lord's introductory words to the first of these seven epistles. All these epistles follow a common plan, setting forth the title, the epistle proper, and the conclusion. In the title of each there is a description of Christ in His Person and work corresponding to the contents of the epistle. In the body of the epistle, Christ's knowledge of the condition of the church, together with praise or reproof of the church in question, is set forth. The conclusion is invariably divided into two parts. In the first three epistles, the first member of the conclusion contains an exhortation to give heed to the words of the Spirit to the churches, and the second member contains the promise to the victors with reference to the completion of Christ's kingdom at His second coming. In the remaining four epistles this order is reversed.

The city of Ephesus, in which this first congregation was founded, was well known, it being the first metropolis of Asia Minor. The congregation there was founded by Paul, who labored there for three years under many difficulties but with great success (cf. Acts 18:19; 20:21; 1 Cor. 15:32; 16:9). It consisted chiefly of heathen converts. After Paul's departure the work in this congregation was carried on by Aquila and Priscilla, Apollos, and subsequently by Timothy. In his farewell address to the Ephesian Elders, Paul forewarned them of dangerous errors which would arise among them (Acts 20:17-29). This prophecy had now been fulfilled. The exalted Lord accordingly sends to them the epistle which follows. The introductory formula, "These things saith He," is characteristic of each of these epistles. This is followed by a designation of the Lord corresponding to the contents of each epistle. In the present epistle the Lord is represented as holding both the pastor and the congregation in His protecting hand, and as walking about among them, and as taking a watchful interest in them and assisting them, as He does in every congregation of His Church. Now follows the message which the Lord sends to this church. As the omniscient Lord, to whom nothing is hid, He begins His message, as in all the epistles that follow, with the words "I know." The first thing that comes under the Lord's observation here is their works in general, the external activity by which their inner life is manifested. All things are naked and open to the all-searching eyes of the Lord. He assures them that He knows their hard labor, their bearing under sufferings and trials and their endurance of them, and their firm steadfastness in their resistance of the antagonism of men of the world toward Christ and His kingdom. The Lord also is fully aware of the zeal of this church and notes their intolerance of those that are evil and the severe test to which they put those who, calling themselves apostles, introduced false teaching as special revelations which they had received. In v. 3 the Lord again takes note of their patient endurance without murmuring or complaining, of all the trials, persecutions, and afflictions that came upon them, and how they endured all this in faithfulness for His name's sake, in steadfast perseverance without growing weary or fainting. For all this the Lord graciously commends them. But, though this congregation possessed so much that was praiseworthy, it was not perfect in the eyes of the Lord. The Lord finds one serious fault with it, the fault of backsliding. He tells them explicitly that there has been a deterioration in this church and that their former zeal for the truth of the Gospel and their love for His cause and kingdom has cooled and is no longer such as it once was. Hence in love He must reprimand them and show them their fault to bring about their amendment. But the Lord is not content merely to censure these people. His censure here lays the foundation for His call to repentance. He calls upon them to remember their former condition and their blessed state in it as they led faithful lives as His children. He earnestly points out to them that the only way in which the relation between the Lord and His church can be restored is by sincere repentance for its departure from its first love, and by performing again its first works. This the Lord strongly urges them to do; and to move them thereto, He adds a threat by way of warning, declaring that He will come to them in judgment and will remove the light of His Gospel from them, if they fail to heed His admonition and do not repent. But the Lord, not desiring to drive them to despair, adds a word of encouragement, saying: "But this thou hast, that thou hatest the deeds of the Nicolaitanes, which I also hate." Just who these Nicolaitanes were is not definitely known; but evidently they were false teachers of a practical character such as Paul prophesied of in Acts 20:30, and may very well be identified with the rising antinomianism (the doctrine that the believing Christian is freed from all claims and obligations of the Moral Law), referred to by Paul in Colossians, by Peter in his Second Epistle, and by Jude. The Lord commends this congregation at Ephesus for its rejection of such errorists and for its repudiation of their works. This epistle closes in v. 7 with a powerful appeal to them to take to heart and give earnest consideration to what has been said in this epistle. This appeal is addressed to each and every one to overcome the temptations of life which beset him on every side. And the Lord's encouraging promise here is that, out of His pure, unmerited grace, He will grant to each overcomer to eat of the tree of life, which is in the midst of the Paradise of God (cf. Gen. 3:24). The reference here is to the heavenly Paradise at God's right hand, where there is joy unspeakable and full of glory and where there are pleasures forevermore. What an incentive ought this promise to be for living a holy, consecrated Christian life in this world! This first of the seven epistles, accompanied, as all Scripture is, by the Spirit of Christ, the Holy Spirit, should be an impressive lesson for all backsliding Christians of every land and of all time.

II. EPISTLE TO THE CHURCH
IN SMYRNA

Chapter 2:8-11

---

8. *And unto the angel of the church in Smyrna write: These things saith the First and the Last, which was dead and is alive: 9. I know thy works and tribulation and poverty (but thou art rich), and I know the blasphemy of them which say they are Jews and are not, but are the synagog of Satan. 10. Fear none of those things which thou shalt suffer. Behold, the devil shall cast some of you into prison that ye may be tried; and ye shall have tribulation ten days. Be thou faithful unto death, and I will give thee a crown of life. 11. He that hath an ear, let him hear what the Spirit saith unto the churches: He that overcometh shall not be hurt of the second death.*

Verse 8 of this chapter gives us the solemn introduction to the Lord's epistle to the church in Smyrna. Like all the rest of these epistles, it is addressed to the congregation through its pastor as its responsible officer. Smyrna, some 40 miles north of Ephesus, was an important place of business on the eastern shore of the Aegean Sea and was a large and beautiful city. The Christian church located there was troubled from without rather than from within. In the opening words of the introduction to this epistle, Christ describes Himself as "the First and the Last," just as in 1:17, thus proclaiming Himself to be the everlasting God. To this He adds as a special reference to His crucifixion and resurrection, "who was dead and is alive." This is an unqualified assertion that He who speaks is the same Christ who suffered on the Cross for the sins of men and who by His own almighty power arose on the third day

to a new life of victory over death, thus becoming the
Source of life to all who believe in Him, and for them
taking from death its sting. In v. 9 the Lord assures this
church that He fully understands its situation and circumstances. He knows its activities; He knows its tribulation,
the afflictions endured by its members for the sake of their
faith and the penalties of imprisonment and death to
which they have been subjected for His sake, and all the
disgrace they have suffered in their faithful service of
their good and gracious Lord. He is also aware of their
deep poverty, due in many cases no doubt to confisca-
tion of their goods in time of persecution. To these poor
people the Lord adds as a word of comfort, "but thou art
rich," thus bringing to them the precious assurance that
as true believers in Him they are rich toward God and
have treasures in heaven which can never be taken away
from them. Another matter pertaining to this church
about which the Lord is concerned and concerning which
He has full and complete knowledge is the blasphemy,
i. e., the evil speaking and slander, of certain men who
claim to be Jews but who in reality are of the synagog
of Satan, who, following the training of their master, are
hostile in their attitude toward Christians. Their gracious
Lord in view of their hard situation gives the members
of this congregation a word of encouragement (v. 10),
assuring them that, although they are suffering, they have
nothing to fear, inasmuch as their almighty Lord is able
to protect them in the most distressing situations they
may encounter. Assuring them that all the afflictions to
which they may be subjected are under His almighty control, He urges them to banish all fear, as nothing can
really harm them. All is under His control, and He will
never leave nor forsake His people in their distresses incurred in His service. The Lord's all-seeing eye, penetrat-

ing into the future, sees the suffering and affliction that lies before this congregation as a consequence of their faithfulness to Him. This sad situation He does not withhold from them. The Lord, who is well aware that the "devil, as a roaring lion, walketh about, seeking whom he may devour," specifically tells them that the devil shall cast some of them into prison. This the Lord Himself will allow, His purpose being that they may be tried, i. e., tested, enabled to prove the reality of their faith and be strengthened therein. Thus the Lord dealt with Abraham; and even so does He test His servants unto this day. "We must through much tribulation enter into the Kingdom of God." For encouragement the Lord adds: "and ye shall have tribulation ten days." Their tribulation will not be long. The Lord has limited the time and made it short and endurable. He is faithful and will not permit them to be tempted beyond their ability to bear it (1 Cor. 10:13). He counsels them to be faithful, however severe their situation may be, to the end of their earthly lives.

As an encouragement to them to do this He gives them an exceedingly precious promise: "and I will give thee a crown of life." This crown He promises to them not because they have deserved it or merited it; but He bestows it alone out of His boundless love and grace. What encouragement is here given to true believers for perseverance in faith under all trials unto the end!

In v. 11 we have the formula for calling attention, which is found in all these epistles. In the closing words of this verse, there occurs another precious promise, which is that the Christian warrior in his faithfulness unto death shall not be hurt of the second death, or in other words, he shall escape the eternal damnation of hell to which the wicked are consigned.

III. EPISTLE TO THE CHURCH
IN PERGAMOS

Chapter 2:12-17

---

12. *And to the angel of the church in Pergamos write: These things saith He which hath the sharp sword with two edges: 13. I know thy works, and where thou dwellest, even where Satan's seat is; and thou holdest fast My name and hast not denied My faith, even in those days wherein Antipas was My faithful martyr, who was slain among you, where Satan dwelleth. 14. But I have a few things against thee, because thou hast there them that hold the doctrine of Balaam, who taught Balac to cast a stumbling block before the children of Israel, to eat things sacrificed unto idols, and to commit fornication. 15. So hast thou also them that hold the doctrine of the Nicolaitanes, which thing I hate. 16. Repent, or else I will come unto thee quickly and will fight against them with the sword of My mouth. 17. He that hath an ear, let him hear what the Spirit saith unto the churches: To him that overcometh will I give to eat of the hidden manna and will give him a white stone, and in the stone a new name written, which no man knoweth saving he that receiveth it.*

---

*V*erse 12 contains the introduction. Christ here describes Himself as having a sharp sword, corresponding to His appearance to John in 1:16 and to the threat He issues in v. 16. This sharp, two-edged sword refers to His Word (cf. Heb. 4:12). In the following verse the Lord testifies to His knowledge of this church in Pergamos, a city noted for its library and for the temple of Aesculapius and as the seat of a Roman supreme court. The Lord fully knows the difficult position in which this church stands, surrounded on all sides by the idolatrous worship, not only of the heathen god Aesculapius, but also of the god of Greek mythology, Zeus Soter. Hence

He describes it as located "where Satan's throne is"; and He knows that this church is beset by many and grievous persecutions. But the Lord also knows that under these exceedingly trying conditions this church holds itself firm and steadfast to the Lord and has not denied its faith in Him. For this He heartily commends the members of this church. He adds as a special commendation to them their faithfulness in the severely testing time when Antipas, His faithful witness, was slain as a martyr among them at the instigation of Satan. Who this Antipas was, whether a bishop of the church at the close of the first century, as has been conjectured, we do not know; but this we do know, that he was Christ's "faithful martyr." And the Lord praises this church that even such a calamity as this did not cause them to lose their faith in Him. This shows the Lord's deep concern for His people in all the trials, temptations, and afflictions that beset them, and His high appreciation of their faithfulness under such untoward circumstances. But no church in this world is perfect. And so Christ deems it necessary to administer a reproof even to this congregation. He has indeed not many, but "a few things" against this church. He charges it with retaining in its membership "them that hold the doctrine of Balaam." Balaam's sin, as described in the book of Numbers, consisted in his counsel to Balak to cause the children of Israel to sin by the seductions of Moabite women to heathen worship with its shameful orgies and vices. Similar sins were in vogue among certain members of the church at Pergamos and were allowed to go unrebuked. Let us ask ourselves in all seriousness whether a similar situation is not found in many of our Christian churches today. This rebuke of the Lord's pertains to them also. But the Lord has still another rebuke to administer to this congregation. He charges it also with tolerating the doctrine of the Nicolai-

tanes — a sect that seduced members of this congregation
to the obscenities of idol worship and to sins of fornication. The holy Lord cannot tolerate such sins among
professing Christians or fail to administer reproof to a
church that does nothing about it. And so immediately
after these charges He addresses to this congregation
a fervid call to repentance. This is precisely the same
message with which the Lord began His public ministry
(cf. Mark 1:15). And to enforce His call to repentance,
the Lord adds the striking threat: "or else I will come
unto thee quickly and will fight against them with the
sword of My mouth."

The Lord cannot look with the least degree of toler-
ance upon sin. His words here give us the threat with
which He enforces His call to repentance. If they repent,
well and good; but if not, the Lord will assuredly visit
them in judgment. In being lax in its discipline and
tolerating such sin among its members, the whole church
is involved in their sin, and hence is included in the
Lord's stern rebuke and in His fervent call to repent.
In v. 17 we have, as at the close of each of the seven
epistles, first the call to attention. This is followed by the
specific promise addressed to the congregation in view of
its pressing needs. This promise is not given to the church
in general or to the church as a whole, but is addressed
to each individual believer who by his faith overcomes
the temptations by which he is beset. To him the Lord
promises a gracious reward, a reward corresponding to
the temptation in which he has shown himself victor.
To every overcomer the Lord promises food, heavenly
manna, described as "hidden" because only in future
glory will it be fully enjoyed (cf. 1 John 3:2). And to
emphasize this still more strongly, the Lord declares that
He will give to each such conqueror a "white stone, and
in the stone a new name written." This name is desig-

nated "new" because its full significance will become
evident only in eternal glory. That the contents of this
stone is known only to him who receives it, is accounted
for by the fact that knowledge of the blessedness of
eternal life is disclosed only in personal experience.

IV. EPISTLE TO THE CHURCH
IN THYATIRA

Chapter 2:18-29

---

18. And unto the angel of the church in Thyatira write: These
things saith the Son of God, who hath His eyes like unto a flame
of fire, and His feet are like fine brass: 19. I know thy works, and
charity, and service, and faith, and thy patience, and thy works;
and the last to be more than the first. 20. Notwithstanding I have
a few things against thee, because thou sufferest that woman
Jezebel, which calleth herself a prophetess, to teach and to seduce
My servants to commit fornication and to eat things sacrificed unto
idols. 21. And I gave her space to repent of her fornication; and
she repented not. 22. Behold, I will cast her into a bed, and them
that commit adultery with her into great tribulation, except they
repent of their deeds. 23. And I will kill her children with death;
and all the churches shall know that I am He which searcheth the
reins and hearts; and I will give unto every one of you according
to your works. 24. But unto you I say, and unto the rest in
Thyatira, as many as have not this doctrine and which have not
known the depths of Satan, as they speak; I will put upon you
none other burden. 25. But that which ye have already hold fast
till I come. 26. And he that overcometh and keepeth my works
unto the end, to him will I give power over the nations; 27. and
He shall rule them with a rod of iron; as the vessels of a potter
shall they be broken to shivers: even as I received of My Father.
28. And I will give him the morning star. 29. He that hath an ear,
let him hear what the Spirit saith unto the churches.

*I*n the first two verses we have the introduction to the epistle to this church. Thyatira was a manufacturing city in Lydia on the road to Sardis. The church here was composed largely of Gentile Christians. In this introduction Christ characterizes Himself, as in 1:13 ff., as the Son of God, who with flaming eyes penetrates everything and with feet of brass treads down all things that are impure and malevolent. The thought to be conveyed is that He, the righteous Judge, will utterly destroy His enemies, who will not be able to stand before Him. In the words that immediately follow He informs this church that everything occurring in it is fully known to Him. "All things are naked and opened unto the eyes of Him with whom we have to do" (Heb. 4:13). In v. 19 the Lord notes four special things among their works, to which He directs attention. The first of these is charity, i. e., love, love toward God and toward the brethren — a genuine fruit of their faith. The second is their faith, of which their patient endurance is a proof. The third is their service, or ministry, as shown in their kindness to the poor and needy. The fourth is their patience under the manifold trials and persecutions which they endured from the hostile world by which they were surrounded. For all these things the Lord commends and approves them, climaxing His commendation by declaring that they were doing more works now than in the beginning of their Christian career. These people were not slipping backward, as is the case with so many Christians today, but were steadily advancing in their Christian course. But notwithstanding the strong praise bestowed upon them, these people were not perfect. The Lord, therefore, brings against them a specific charge in v. 20. He tells them that they are enduring a notorious sinner among them without reproving or rebuking her for her evil deeds or her pernicious influence. This woman

He calls Jezebel because of her resemblance in character to the wicked wife of King Ahab (1 Kings 16:31; 2 Kings 9:32).

The Lord vividly depicts the nature of this wicked woman who proclaimed herself a prophetess, who taught that Christians should overcome their carnal lusts by yielding to and indulging in them to the full; and also that, to gain influence with the heathen, they should join with them in their idolatrous feasts. With this notoriously evil woman the Lord declares that He showed Himself patient, extending to her the time of grace in order to afford her space for repentance. But she, as is the case with so many today, obstinately refused to repent of her specific sin, the sin of fornication. The Lord here censures this congregation for allowing her to continue in their midst and for doing nothing to remove this moral blotch from them. In v. 22 He solemnly pronounces His threat, which will be executed without fail in case of disobedience. Here He expressly asserts that her bed of sensuality will be turned into a bed of sickness and that her sins will be visited upon her even in this life. And to this He adds that He will also visit punishment upon her followers who have been seduced by her into shameful sins of lewdness; but at the same time the good and gracious Lord holds out hope for such sinners. If they repent and forsake the deeds into which they have been led by this vile woman, the Lord will still show Himself gracious and will not execute His threat upon them.

In v. 23 the Lord indicates the punishment which is to be meted out for the sin of adultery. This He declares will be fully carried out in the utter extermination of this woman's followers, or children. This is a solemn warning not only to this congregation, but to all other congregations as well; and it shows us that no sin, however secret it may be, is hidden from the all-seeing eyes of the Lord.

This definitely shows that no transgressor can possibly escape the Lord's notice or His avenging justice. The omniscient Lord, who searches the deepest recesses of the heart with His ever-watchful eye, will visit merited punishment upon the most secret forms of sin and will punish transgressors in full measure in proportion to their wicked works (cf. Gal. 6:7-8).

In v. 24 and the verses that follow to the end of this chapter, the Lord addresses the Christians in the church at Thyatira who had not yielded to the seductions of the false prophetess, but who had remained faithful to Him. To the true Christians, His faithful followers, who kept themselves aloof from this libertinism (unrestrained indulgence in lewd practices), "the deep things of Satan, as they speak," the Lord addresses an encouraging promise. In His deep care and concern for them He assures them that He will lay upon them no further burden of suffering than that which they have already borne. But in the succeeding verse He admonishes them to be on their guard, inasmuch as they still have the same burdens to bear which they have previously borne. Consequently He urges them to steadfastness and perseverance in their Christian lives unto the end, or until Christ Himself comes. In the passage vv. 26-29 the Lord addresses a gracious promise to His faithful followers. This is addressed to the church collectively, but also to each individual who overcomes the assaults of the devil, the world, and his own flesh, and keeps unto the end the works enjoined upon him by his Lord. This promise in substance is that every such one shall be made partaker of Christ's own glory and power. Just as Christ rules over the nations and subdues all enemies under His feet, so shall believers judge the world at the side of Jesus Christ, their Lord. And in His further promise of "the morning star" the Lord gives expression to the exceeding brightness of the heavenly glory with which each victor will be endowed. This epistle the Lord closes, as He does the others, with a mighty call to Christians not to forget the urgent admonitions and the glorious promises of their Lord, but ever to bear them in mind. Surely the message in this epistle is one that we all should take to heart. Let us diligently meditate upon it.

V. EPISTLE TO THE CHURCH
IN SARDIS

Chapter 3:1-6

---

1. *And unto the angel of the church in Sardis write: These things saith He that hath the seven Spirits of God and the seven stars: I know thy works, that thou hast a name that thou livest and art dead.* 2. *Be watchful, and strengthen the things which remain, that are ready to die; for I have not found thy works perfect before God.* 3. *Remember, therefore, how thou hast received and heard, and hold fast, and repent. If, therefore, thou shalt not watch, I will come on thee as a thief, and thou shalt not know what hour I will come upon thee.* 4. *Thou hast a few names even in Sardis which have not defiled their garments; and they shall walk with Me in white; for they are worthy.* 5. *He that overcometh, the same shall be clothed in white raiment; and I will not blot out his name out of the Book of Life, but I will confess his name before My Father and before His angels.* 6. *He that hath an ear, let him hear what the Spirit saith unto the churches.*

---

*I*n the first verse of this chapter we have the introduction to the epistle to the church in Sardis. This city, thirty miles south of Thyatira, was a prosperous manufacturing city, the ancient capital of

Croesus, the wealthy king of Lydia, whose empire was overthrown by Cyrus the Great. The Lord, fully knowing the sad condition of this congregation, suffering, as it was, from spiritual deadness, sends His brief but stirring message to this congregation. He describes Himself here as having "the seven Spirits of God," i. e., the Holy Spirit, whom He sends, through whom He works, and through whom He speaks in and to the churches. And since the Holy Spirit works only through the Word, and since the Word is committed officially to the ministry symbolized in the seven stars (cf. 1:16; 2:1), the Lord represents Himself here as having "the seven stars." This implies that the pastor of this church is under the control of the Lord Jesus Christ, and so under responsibility to render account to Him for the conditions in this parish entrusted to his care. We should remember here that the Lord as Head of the Church is the Lord of every single congregation in it, and that, while He protects and shields His ministers, He holds them to strict account in the carrying on of the great work which He has entrusted to them. The Lord now declares that He knows the works of this congregation with all its imperfections and defects. He tells them that this church, while it has the reputation among men of being an active, wide-awake church, is such only in its outward appearance. And to bring it to a realization of its actual condition, He pronounces upon it, sharply and clearly: "thou art dead." It had in its membership only a few true believers who were actually united with their Lord. And how true this is of many churches today — many professing Christians, but few real believers! Wherever there is faith, it will inevitably find expression in life; and profession without performance is mere hypocrisy and as such incurs the stern condemnation of the Lord (cf. Matt. 7:21-22; 23:27).

In vv. 2 and 3 the Lord addresses His admonitions to this church. The first of these is called forth by the sad spiritual state of the majority of its members, whom He has just pronounced dead. It is a powerful call not only to arouse it out of its spiritual slumbers, but also to be on the alert in strengthening or establishing the rest of the things which are on the 'verge of dying. This calls for strong measures on the part of the faithful to succor this church from succumbing to complete death. They must be up and doing if they are to give new life to this church which is about to die. As a reason for this stirring admonition and for their yielding uncompromising obedience to it, the Lord declares that He has not found their works perfect in the sight of God. Their works are formal and empty, mere outward performances, as is the case in many congregations today. Faith, love, and spiritual life have not characterized their activities. The trouble with this church is not persecution from without, or heresy from within, but that its life is in a decadent state, or already dead. As they realize their real condition, they should be moved to give earnest heed to this admonition of the Lord. The Lord now addresses to them a second admonition, reminding them of their past experience as a Christian congregation and pleading with them to recall the eagerness with which they in the beginning had received and heard the Gospel of divine grace which had been preached to them. He does this in order to induce them to hold fast and keep the divine truth which they had then received and to repent, and thus cleanse, strengthen, and perfect the new life which had been implanted in them by the power of the Word. As a reinforcement to this admonition the Lord adds an impressive warning, viz., that in case they fail to heed the admonition to be on their guard and to repent, the Lord will come in judgment upon them, surely, suddenly, and

unexpectedly. So sudden and so unexpected will this
be, that they will not realize at what hour the judgment
will strike them. This special judgment upon them does
not exclude the Lord's coming for final Judgment, but is
a type of it.

In v. 4 the Lord notes certain exceptions to the general sinfulness prevailing in this congregation. In it there
were a few members who did not approve of, or partici-
pate in, the sin that characterized this church as a whole.
These few were sincere faithful Christians who were
leading pure, wholesome Christian lives in the midst of
the prevailing corruption. The Lord, who always gladly
acknowledges the good wherever it is to be found, gives
to these faithful ones an exceedingly precious promise to
encourage them in their steadfastness. This promise is
that they shall walk in company with their Lord in white
robes, symbolical of heavenly holiness (cf. 4:4; 6:11; 7:9;
19:8). To this promise the Lord adds an expression of
His own estimate of these saints in the words "for they
are worthy." This worthiness the Lord pronounces upon
them, not because of their righteous works, but because
of their faith, of which their lives give such rich evidence.
The Lord's grace was not bestowed upon them in vain,
but was effective in keeping their lives clean unto the
end, and that in spite of the manifold temptations by
which they were confronted. What an assurance here
that the Lord will never fail His faithful followers!

In v. 5 we have the Lord's gracious promise to this
congregation. This promise, as in all the other epistles,
is not a general one, but is individualized and is given to
every one who by the grace of God conquers, or overcomes, in all the temptations of life that beset him. The
substance of this promise is that every Christian who
overcomes in the great battle against Satan with all his

wiles shall by the grace of Christ be arrayed in the white,
spotless garment of Christ's perfect righteousness, all the
stains of his sins being washed away in the blood of the
Lamb. To this He adds for further comfort and consolation: "and I will not blot out his name out of the Book
of Life." This is, of course, figurative language but thor-
oughly Scriptural (cf. Ex. 32:32; Ps. 69:28; Dan. 12:1;
et al.). The Book of Life is the infallible record of the
Lord's omniscience. This book contains the names of all
true believers of all time. Christ's definite promise to the
conquering one is that He will not erase his name from
the Book of Life, but that it shall remain in this book to
all eternity. This is to him the assurance of eternal life
with his Lord in heaven. And to this the Lord adds as
a climax: "I will confess his name before My Father and
before His angels." This is a precious assurance to every
true believer that, when God's wrath strikes the unbelievers on the day of final Judgment, He who is the believer's Redeemer, Savior, and Lord will acknowledge
him as his very own and that he will be eternally saved.
What an encouragement to the true believer this is to
fight the good fight of faith to the end of his earthly
career! The Lord now closes this epistle in the same
words as in the others with a call to attention, admonish-
ing each member to give due heed to all that their Lord
has said in this epistle, with the full assurance that it is
the Spirit of God who is here speaking to them through
the words of their Lord.

VI. EPISTLE TO THE CHURCH
IN PHILADELPHIA

Chapter 3:7-13

---

7. And to the angel of the church in Philadelphia write: These things saith He that is holy, He that is true, He that hath the key of David, He that openeth, and no man shutteth; and shutteth, and no man openeth: 8. I know thy works; behold, I have set before thee an open door, and no man can shut it; for thou hast a little strength and hast kept My Word and hast not denied My name. 9. Behold, I will make them of the synagog of Satan which say they are Jews and are not, but do lie, behold, I will make them to come and worship before thy feet and to know that I have loved thee. 10. Because thou hast kept the Word of My patience, I also will keep thee from the hour of temptation, which shall come upon all the world to try them that dwell upon the earth. 11. Behold, I come quickly; hold that fast which thou hast, that no man take thy crown. 12. Him that overcometh will I make a pillar in the temple of My God, and he shall go no more out; and I will write upon him the name of My God and the name of the city of My God, which is new Jerusalem, which cometh down out of heaven from My God; and I will write upon him My new name. 13. He that hath an ear, let him hear what the Spirit saith unto the churches.

The city of Philadelphia derived its name from its founder, King Attalus Philadelphus.

In the introduction (v. 7) the Lord designates Himself as the Holy One whose holiness is absolute and who as having "the key of David" is divine in the fullest sense of the term (cf. John 6:69), and also as the "True One," true in the same sense as it applies to God (cf. John 14:6). The final words of the introduction: "He that openeth, and no man shutteth; and shutteth, and no man openeth," are explanatory of what is involved in the key of David. It pictures the Lord as the absolute Master in His kingdom with full power to admit into it and to exclude from it. With this power of the Lord no man can interfere. This power the Lord indeed does delegate to others in His Church; but it is only by His power and according to His Word that they may open and close (cf. John 20:21-23).

In the beginning of the epistle proper (v. 8) the Lord testifies to His knowledge of this church and of everything that occurs in it and includes here a word of commendation of this church as being a true, faithful, and successful church. Here He states parenthetically that He has in His providence set before this church an open door. This is a reference to the missionary opportunities afforded to this congregation. Of what is meant by the "open door" we have an illustration in Acts 16:9, where Paul, after being excluded from Bithynia, had a door opened to him to preach the Gospel in Macedonia. Just so is a door here opened to the church in Philadelphia, which no opposition on the part of man can close or shut. This, as the context shows, was an opportunity to do mission work among the Jews. The Lord in setting before this congregation its opportunity for service on His behalf encourages it, adding three things by way of commendation. The first point here is that this congregation has "a little strength." This refers not to any lack of spiritual strength on the part of these Christians, but to the numerical strength of this congregation, it being small in numbers and probably also lacking in social prominence. Such being its situation, it would naturally be inclined to undertake little; but the Lord here assures them that, even though they are small in numbers, He can make use of them and that He keeps the door wide open to them. The second point in the Lord's commendation of them is that they did not yield to the temptations of the world, the flesh, and the devil; nor were they influenced by the opposition of unbelievers to turn away from Christ's Word, but kept it in their hearts and consistently taught and preached it (cf. John 14:15, 23-24). The final point in the commendation, which stands in close connection with the preceding, is that they did not deny His name, i. e., His revelation, or fail to confess Him (cf. Rom. 10:9-10).

In v. 9 the Lord calls special attention to the fact that in their carrying on of His work He will not forsake them, but will see to it that they are successful. The Lord indicates in this passage that those whom He gives to them as objects of their missionary efforts are not false Christians, but Jews. In describing them as "the synagog of Satan," and in the words that follow, the Lord implies that these are not true Jews in spite of their claim to be such, but because of their enmity toward Him and their rejection of Him as their true Messiah, they are actually liars (cf. what Paul says in Rom. 2:29). But notwithstanding their deplorable condition, their state is not altogether hopeless. The Lord gives assurance to this congregation, in connection with their mission work among the Jews, that He will draw some who will come into the Christian Church and worship Jesus Christ as the true Messiah and that their work will not be in vain among these people. The Lord further assures them that these Jewish converts will realize that His love rested upon the Church and, now that they are converted, rests upon them also. In the verse that follows the Lord gives to this Christian congregation the precious assurance that inasmuch as they have kept the Word of His patience, i. e., the Word that deals with the suffering Messiah, the center of all Scripture, He will keep them out of the im-

pending trial which is to come on all the earth dwellers.
A signal favor on the Lord's part to this faithful church!

In v. 11 there is a statement frequently occurring in
Revelation in reference to the coming of the Lord (cf.
Rev. 22:7, 12, 20). His coming is introduced here for the
encouragement and consolation of believers. It must not
be limited exclusively to the second coming of the Lord,
but includes all preceding judgments. The Lord will
make no delay: His words here are intended to keep believers in a constant state of expectancy of their Lord's
coming. The unbelieving world in the days of the Apostles and ever since has scoffed at the idea of the second
coming of the Lord (2 Pet. 3:4); but Peter's answer still
holds good, that God is not slack concerning His promise,
but long-suffering (2 Pet. 3:8 f.). In view of the certainty
and suddenness of His coming, the gracious Lord gives to
this faithful church an impressive exhortation to persevere
and keep its faith unto the end. He assures them that
nothing less is at stake than the crown of eternal life and
blessedness, which He has promised to them that endure.
For us today this is an equally solemn admonition. By
sinking into a false security we are likewise in danger of
losing that which we have (1 Cor. 10:12). Since the devil,
the world, and our own flesh are ever active in seeking
to deprive us of our crown, we have all the more reason
to heed the Lord's admonition to hold fast that which we
have. To encourage the conquering one in this matter,
the Lord adds (v. 12) an exceedingly precious promise,
declaring that He will make him a pillar in the temple of
His God, which means that he will have a permanent
place in the Kingdom of Glory in the presence of God.
This heavenly abode, the Lord further assures him, he
will never leave either voluntarily as by a fall or under
the constraint of any outside sources whatever. He thus
indicates that this holy and blessed state will be his for-

ever and ever. The further description of the "New Jerusalem," the Eternal City (21:3), in figurative language beyond our conception or ability of expression has significance similar to the first figure and carries the same assurance. The same may be said of Christ's new name, of which He says in 19:12 that no man knows it but He Himself. All these names united in proclaiming the Lord Jesus Christ as the eternal King of the Kingdom of Heaven. In v. 13, we have precisely the same call to attention that is found at the end of all these epistles. In it each church is called upon to hearken to the words which the Holy Spirit addresses to it, whether by way of warning and rebuke or by way of commendation and encouragement. It is noteworthy that in this epistle there is not one word of censure from the Lord. What an inspiring example this church sets for our Christian congregations of today!

VII. EPISTLE TO THE CHURCH
IN LAODICEA

Chapter 3:14-22

---

14. *And unto the angel of the church of the Laodiceans write: These things saith the Amen, the faithful and true Witness, the Beginning of the creation of God:* 15. *I know thy works, that thou art neither cold nor hot; I would thou wert cold or hot.* 16. *So, then, because thou art lukewarm and neither cold nor hot, I will spue thee out of My mouth.* 17. *Because thou sayest, I am rich, and increased with goods, and have need of nothing; and knowest not that thou art wretched, and miserable, and poor, and blind, and naked.* 18. *I counsel thee to buy of Me gold tried in the fire that thou mayest be rich, and white raiment, that thou mayest be clothed and that the shame of thy nakedness do not appear; and*

anoint thine eyes with eyesalve, that thou mayest see. 19. As many as I love, I rebuke and chasten; be zealous, therefore, and repent. 20. Behold, I stand at the door and knock; if any man hear My voice and open the door, I will come in to him and will sup with him, and he with Me. 21. To him that overcometh will I grant to sit with Me in My throne, even as I also overcame and am set down with My Father in His throne. 22. He that hath an ear, let him hear what the Spirit saith unto the churches.

---

*L*aodicea, located about 50 miles from Philadelphia, was the capital of Phrygia. It was renowned as a rich manufacturing and commercial city. The Christian church there is mentioned by Paul in Col. 4:16.

In the introduction to this epistle, Christ speaks of Himself as the "Amen," which He at once explains by the words "the faithful and true Witness." This attests the fact that all that He says is the eternal truth and trustworthy beyond all question. Christ is "not man that He should lie or the son of man that He should repent." To this He adds: "the Beginning of the creation of God." To understand these words to mean that Christ is the first creature created by God would be contrary to all Scripture teaching concerning Christ as well as to Rev. 1:8; 2:18; and John 1:3. They really designate Him as the active source of God's universe, or the absolute medium of the whole creation, which exists only in reference to Him (cf. Col. 1:15-18).

In v. 15 the Lord unqualifiedly asserts that the works of this congregation, which bear evidence of its inward condition, are well known to Him. These professing Christians may deceive themselves, but they cannot deceive the Lord. He knows that this congregation as a whole is in a lukewarm condition, "neither cold nor hot." The word "cold" refers to the unconverted who has never

been touched by the warmth of the Gospel. The word
"hot," on the other hand, refers to one who has been converted and has become an ardent believer who cleaves to
his Lord with fervent love. We are reminded of a similar
saying of the Savior: "He that is not with Me is against
Me" (Matt. 12:30). One is either hot or cold, with or
against Jesus. Lukewarmness, tepidity, and indifference
toward the Savior is tantamount to opposition to and
denial of Jesus. When the Lord says to this church: "I will
spue thee out of My mouth," He does not state something
that is sure to take place, but something that will un-
avoidably occur unless there is a decisive change in the
congregation's attitude toward Him. Although His judgment is about to come, room is still left for repentance.
This church may yet obey His call. A possibility is still
open for averting His judgment; and the whole purpose
of His threat is to bring about such a state of repentance.

In vv. 17-18 the Lord also lays bare the false claims
which this church makes for itself and gives counsel for
its enlightenment and guidance. This church is represented here as proudly boasting of its spiritual possessions
and gifts and as claiming to be rich to such an extent that
it no longer stands in need of anything. In its own
estimation it is self-sufficient; and with a proud Pharisaical
spirit it looks down upon other churches as possessing an
impoverished Christianity in comparison with it. The
spirit of humility is entirely wanting in the members of
this congregation. The Lord consequently clearly unveils
before them their real condition and sharply exposes their
utter self-deception. Instead of being rich, as they thought
and claimed to be, He declares that they are in a distressing condition, worthy of pity, having the cringing
attitude of a beggar, unable to see, and without clothes
to cover their shame. Such is actually the condition of

this church, ignorant though it is of it. In view of their deplorable condition the Lord does not address to them harsh censure or strict commands, as might be expected; but, just as the Gospel does, of which He is the embodiment, He advises them in a most friendly way. His first counsel is that they buy of Him gold tried in the fire, i. e., pure gold, refined and free from all alloy. The figure here represents the righteousness of Christ, which is imputed to true faith. To buy this of Him means to obtain it freely by His grace (cf. Is. 55:1). This earnest counsel shows how deeply concerned the Lord is for the salvation of the souls of those whom He is addressing, and also of all souls whom He has redeemed at so great a cost to Himself. The second gracious counsel of the Lord to this congregation deals with the white robes with which they are to be clothed. These white robes are symbolical of the righteousness of Christ that is imputed to each believer (Matt. 22:11). White is always the symbol of holiness. The purpose of this is, that the shame of their nakedness may not appear. The third counsel to this congregation is to buy eyesalve that it may really see. This figure refers to the illumination which the Holy Spirit bestows through the Word, whereby true spiritual sight is created.

In v. 19 the Lord asserts His love for this congregation as a whole. He loves all its members, not only the faithful ones, but also the unfaithful whom He has just rebuked as unworthy of His love. He assures them that He does not rebuke and chasten in wrath or anger, but in love. However grievous His chastenings may be, they are intended to work in the recipients the wholesome fruits of righteousness; and they are evidences of His concern for them and of His love toward them. This is manifest in His earnest admonition to them not merely to repent, but to be zealous in their repentance. The Lord who

came into the world to save sinners will leave nothing
undone to secure their eternal salvation.

In v. 20 He gives a vivid picture of Himself, the Savior
of mankind, as standing at the door of each sinner's heart
and knocking for admittance. Thereby He brings home
to this careless, lukewarm church the fact of His constant
presence, which it was so prone to forget. What a precious truth this is not only for the Laodiceans of so long
ago, but for all men even in our day, wherever the Gospel
is preached and the Sacraments are administered! And
His precious promise still holds good, that if anyone hear
His voice and open the door, He will enter into the closest
and most intimate communion with him — a communion
that will be mutually enjoyed. While it is quite true that
the sinner cannot open the door by his own powers, this
power is brought to him through the voice of the Lord,
the Gospel of Christ, which is the power of God unto salvation (Rom. 1:16). This coming is not to be confused
with the second coming of Christ to receive His own unto
Himself, but is a coming here and now, a feasting with
Christ, which will find its consummation in the blessed
fellowship of heaven to all eternity (cf. John 14:23;
1 John 2:24).

In v. 21 we have the Lord's gracious promise. It is
addressed, as in all these epistles, to the individual who
by God's grace fights the good fight of faith and overcomes. The promise here, unlike that in the preceding
verse, is eschatological, pertaining to the future in the
kingdom of heaven. It is implied here also that this is
a gift of pure grace on the part of the Lord to which the
conquering one contributes nothing whatever. It closes
with an historical reference to Christ's victorious death
on the Cross and His subsequent exaltation to God's right
hand in majesty, dominion, and power. Just as surely as

Christ overcame and is set down on His Father's throne, just so surely shall the conquering believer share in the glory and bliss of heaven (cf. Rev. 2:7; 22:5). Surely such a promise as this should move us away from complacency and lead us to zealous repentance and to joyful trust in our most gracious and loving Lord, who leaves nothing undone to secure our final salvation. "Thanks be unto God for His unspeakable Gift!"

This epistle concludes, as is the case with all the others, with an earnest appeal to this lukewarm church to give diligent heed to the Lord's call to repent and to embrace in faith the precious promises He holds out to them.

Part Two

REVELATION CONCERNING
THE CONSUMMATION OF
GOD'S KINGDOM

CHAPTERS 4 TO 22

†

Chapter 4

1. After this I looked, and, behold, a door was opened in heaven; and the first voice which I heard was as it were of a trumpet talking with me, which said: Come up higher, and I will show thee things which must be hereafter. 2. And immediately I was in the spirit; and, behold, a throne was set in heaven, and One sat on the throne. 3. And He that sat was to look upon like a jasper and a sardine stone; and there was a rainbow round about the throne, in sight like unto an emerald. 4. And round about the throne were four and twenty seats; and upon the seats I saw four and twenty elders sitting, clothed in white raiment; and they had on their heads crowns of gold. 5. And out of the throne proceeded lightnings and thunderings and voices; and there were seven lamps of fire burning before the throne, which are the seven Spirits of God. 6. And before the throne there was a sea of glass like unto crystal; and in the midst of the throne and round about the throne were four living ones full of eyes before and behind. 7. And the first living one was like a lion, and the second living one like a calf, and the third living one had a face as a man, and the fourth living one was like a flying eagle. 8. And the four living ones had each of them six wings about him; and they were full of eyes within; and they rest not day and night, saying: Holy, holy, holy, Lord God Almighty, which was, and is, and is to come. 9. And when those living ones give glory and honor and thanks to Him that sat on the throne, who liveth forever and ever, 10. the four and twenty elders fall down before Him that sat on the throne, and worship Him that liveth forever and ever, and cast their crowns before the throne, saying: 11. Thou art worthy, O Lord, to receive glory and honor and power; for Thou hast created all things, and for Thy pleasure they are and were created.

49

*T*he expression "after these things" (v. 1) refers
back to what has preceded from 1:10 to the
close of Chapter 3 and marks the sequence of what John
saw. John is still "in the spirit" and continues in this state
throughout the whole revelation which he records in this
book. The words "I saw" with which he introduces the
present vision mark a peculiar feature of this revelation.
What John saw in this vision was a door that had been
opened and was still standing wide open, disclosing the
interior of heaven. The voice to which John here refers
was the voice of the Lord Jesus, the same voice of which
he has spoken in 1:10. In his description of this voice as
the voice, as it were, of a trumpet talking with him, he
designates this voice as clear, ringing, penetrating, and
majestic. The first words of this voice, "Come up hither,"
are a summons to John not merely to look in through the
open door, but to enter therein and behold things close
at hand. The words that follow in this verse are in fulfillment of Christ's promise in 1:1. The things which John is
to be shown in the visions that follow are symbols exhibiting realities in a veiled way, concealing from us that
which is beyond our ken.

In v. 2 John indicates his compliance with the summons of his Lord. It was "in the spirit" that John obeyed
this command. How this occurred, "whether in the body
or out of the body," we do not know, and perhaps even
John himself did not know (cf. 2 Cor. 12:2-4). The word
"behold" directs attention to the marvelousness of the
vision that was granted John to see. It was nothing less
than a throne placed in heaven and One sitting upon it.
This heavenly throne, far above all earthly, finite thrones,
represents infinite dominion, authority, and power. And
the One sitting upon it is represented as reigning over the
universe, exercising in infinite measure His dominion,
authority, and power.

In the next verse John gives us a vivid description of the "One sitting upon the throne," comparing Him in His brilliant radiance to two of the most precious stones of the earth, "jasper," probably diamond, and "sardius," or carnelian, a red, flesh-colored gem of striking brilliance. In addition to this John sees in the vision a rainbow of emerald green surrounding the throne, symbolizing the grace of God. This rainbow is symbolical of God's peaceful rule on the earth (cf. Luke 2:14). This is a fundamental vision and affords great comfort to believers, with whom He that sitteth upon the throne is well pleased.

In v. 4 John continues his description of what he saw in this vision. Round about God's throne just described John sees twenty-four "seats," literally, "thrones," and on these thrones twenty-four elders sitting. The power of these thrones is derived from the throne of God with which they are intimately connected and closely associated. On these thrones John sees twenty-four elders seated. The term "elder" as used in the New Testament is a designation of the ministry of the Word. Their sitting on these thrones symbolizes the exercise of power — the power which comes through the Word of God committed to the ministry, and by which it rules to the glory of God in the hearts of believers; and in the world, by the judgment which it visits upon unbelievers (John 12:48). The number twenty-four is symbolic of the Church of the Old Testament with its twelve Patriarchs and of the Church of the New Testament with its twelve Apostles. The elders as well as the thrones are symbolical. This excludes all reference to elders serving in heaven, or to martyrs, or other notables among God's people on earth transferred to heavenly glory. Hence no personal names are assigned to them; but as symbolical figures they are without names. Their being clothed in white raiment symbolizes their heavenly holiness. The throne described in v. 5, is the throne of Almighty God, which symbolizes His eternal power and dominion. So mighty a throne cannot but have tremendous manifestations. Hence out of this throne, John declares, proceeded lightnings, voices, and thunders, symbolic manifestations of God's omnipotent rule. Besides, John sees in this vision seven lamps, or torches of fire, burning before the throne of God. These torches symbolize the seven Spirits of God, or in other words the Holy Spirit, and characterize Him as illuminating, seeing, and searching all things (cf. 1:14).

In the following verse John proceeds to give further description of this vision. In speaking of the sea of glass before this throne, he does not refer to spatial relations, which do not apply to heaven, but only to its relation to the throne; and in describing it as clear as crystal, he refers not to its unruffled smoothness, but solely to its radiant transparency. This imagery represents the providence of God, which, though often dark to men and full of mysteries, is seen in heaven in all its brilliant clearness. In the following words in this verse, God's providential rule and dominion are represented as radiating from a center in an unbroken circle. Many solutions have been offered as to who "the four living ones" are. Some regard them as angels. Others regard them as angels of the highest rank, such as cherubim or seraphim, referring to Old Testament passages in Ezekiel and Isaiah; but this is excluded by Rev. 5:11, where the living ones are mentioned alongside the angels and the twenty-four elders in such a way as to exclude their inclusion in either of these classes or their identification with them. Another opinion advanced, that these living ones represent the four Evangelists: St. Matthew the man, St. Mark the lion, St. Luke the ox, and St. John the eagle, has nothing to support it and is imaginary and wholly fanciful. We cannot identify these living ones with any known creatures. We must bear in mind that it is a vision that is here described; and that these living ones are symbolical, portraying the earthly agencies of God's providence, the number four indicating the world in which God's providence reigns unceasingly until the end of time. The fact that these living ones are depicted as "full of eyes before and behind," symbolizes their ability to see in every direction so as to carry out God's providential plans and purposes in all their multitudinous details.

In v. 7 a description of each of these living ones is given. The first living one is here likened unto a lion. This symbolizes the royal power and majesty of Jesus Christ, "the Lion of the tribe of Judah, through whose Word and Spirit believers are made kings and priests before Him." The second living one is likened unto a young ox (calf, A. V.). This symbolizes patience — the patience of Jesus Christ as exhibited in His supreme sacrifice, whereby He gave His body unto death for the sins of the world. The third living one is described as having the face of a human being. This symbolizes the human descent of Jesus Christ, who was made like unto us, sin alone excepted. The fourth living one is likened unto a flying eagle. This symbolizes soaring majesty and emphasizes the divine origin of Christ and His return to God. Here not the eagle alone, but also the flying is significant.

A description of these four living ones follows in v. 8. The number four indicates, as we have seen, the world in which God's providence reigns. These four living ones are the immediate agencies of God's providence, in whom God's rule and dominion radiates. These living ones are further described as full of eyes round about and within; and it is to these eyes to which significance is attached. It should be noted that it is not the wings, but the living ones that have the eyes; also that the term "within" does not refer to eyes underneath the wings. The large number of eyes is significant. These eyes are for the purpose of seeing and are indicative of the constant watchfulness with which these living ones observe the throne of God and see whither they go in the execution of His providential will. As "within" they are directed toward the continual observance of the Lord and His providential purposes. As "round about," they are directed toward the execution of God's purposes on things without; and in connection with the mention of the wings, they indicate swiftness in the execution of God's plans. And the statement that they have no rest day and night sets forth their unceasing activity, thus showing that they are never idle in the service of their God. The closing words of this verse contain the utterance of these living ones — an ascription of praise addressed to the Triune God, corresponding to the *Trisagion* in Is. 6:3. This ascription of praise to the Lord God Almighty comes from the lips of these living ones as representatives of His creatures, who are in duty bound to render to Him unceasing praise. The attribute of holiness here ascribed to God is both immanent in God and active toward His creatures, whom He would make holy and upon whom He would bestow salvation.

In v. 9 the doxology in v. 8 is explained as consisting in the giving of glory, honor, and thanksgiving to the Lord God, the Almighty. By this is meant that they acknowledge His glory, i. e., the sum of all His attributes; that they render Him the reverence that is His due; and that they give thanks to Him for all that He does. In the description of Him as sitting on the throne and as living forever and ever, we have an explanation of what is involved in the last words of v. 8, "Lord God Almighty, which was, and is, and is to come." It is to this Divine

Being, ever living, ever active, that the living ones ascribe all praise, honor, and thanksgiving.

In v. 10 we have a description of the action of the twenty-four elders (see v. 4). These elders are purely symbolical and are the agents of the Word in the same manner as the four living ones are the agents of God's providence. They are represented here as falling down before Him in worshipful adoration and as casting their crowns before His throne as a sign of their deep humility in the presence of their King and Lord.

In the last verse of this chapter is given the expression of praise which these elders render to God, the Creator of all things, who brought all things into existence by His own will and for His own pleasure. This first vision is fundamental for all that follows and teaches a lesson that we all should learn and take seriously to heart.

Chapter 5

1. *And I saw in the right hand of Him that sat on the throne a book written within and on the back side, sealed with seven seals.* 2. *And I saw a strong angel proclaiming with a loud voice: Who is worthy to open the book and to loose the seals thereof?* 3. *And no man in heaven nor in earth, neither under the earth, was able to open the book, neither to look thereon.* 4. *And I wept much because no man was found worthy to open and to read the book, neither to look thereon.* 5. *And one of the elders saith unto me: Weep not; behold, the Lion of the tribe of Juda, the Root of David, hath prevailed to open the book and to loose the seven seals thereof.* 6. *And I beheld, and, lo, in the midst of the throne and of the four living ones, and in the midst of the elders, stood a Lamb as it had been slain, having seven horns and seven eyes, which are the seven Spirits of God sent forth into all the earth.*

7. *And He came and took the book out of the right hand of Him that sat upon the throne. 8. And when He had taken the book, the four living ones and four and twenty elders fell down before the Lamb, having every one of them harps and golden vials full of odors, which are the prayers of saints. 9. And they sung a new song, saying: Thou art worthy to take the book and to open the seals thereof; for Thou wast slain and hast redeemed us to God by Thy blood out of every kindred and tongue and people and nation; 10. and hast made us unto our God kings and priests: and we shall reign on the earth. 11. And I beheld, and I heard the voice of many angels round about the throne and the living ones and the elders; and the number of them was ten thousand times ten thousand and thousands of thousands; 12. saying with a loud voice: Worthy is the Lamb that was slain to receive power, and riches, and wisdom, and strength, and honor, and glory, and blessing. 13. And every creature which is in heaven, and on the earth, and under the earth, and such as are in the sea, and all that are in them, heard I saying: Blessing, and honor, and glory, and power be unto Him that sitteth upon the throne and unto the Lamb forever and ever. 14. And the four living ones said: Amen. And the four and twenty elders fell down and worshiped Him that liveth forever and ever.*

The first verse of this chapter introduces a new vision. The preceding vision was a vision of the throne. The present vision is a vision of the Lamb. The things common to each are the throne and He that sitteth upon it, the twenty-four elders and the four living ones. The introductory words, "And I saw," mark this as an entirely new vision. What John saw now follows. That which he saw, he tells us, was a book in the right hand of Him that sat on the throne. What is remarkable about this book is that it was so securely sealed — not with a single seal, but with seven seals. This effective sealing indicates the importance of this book. It is not an ordinary book, but a book containing a full, complete, and perfect record of God's gracious dealing with the world

in the establishment of His kingdom upon earth. The
whole record of all that must occur is known to God,
and to Him alone. Only so much of it becomes known as
God Himself wills; and this is released in revealing symbolism, as each seal is successively broken. The book itself is not read at all; but with the opening of each seal
a vision is revealed to John. These visions are recorded
in succession by him in Revelation from Chapter 6 to the
end of this wonderful book.

In vv. 2-3 John further states what he saw in this
vision, viz., an angel. This was not an ordinary angel, but
a strong angel with a powerful voice. The proclamation
of this mighty angel was: "Who is worthy to open the
book and to loose its seals?" This means to say that no
creature, whether man or angel, has the power or ability
to open the book by unfastening its seals. This is emphatically brought out in v. 3, where it is expressly declared that no personal created being in the universe
could open the book or look upon its contents.

V. 4 gives John's reaction to this fact. He tells us:
"And I wept much," literally, "And I was weeping much."
Considerable speculation is indulged in as to why John
should thus weep. The most probable reason is that this
book would remain sealed forever and that its contents
would never be known.

In the following verse we see John's grief is appeased.
One of the elders, who, as we have seen, are representatives and ministers of the Word, admonishes him not to
weep and brings to him the comfort that he so sorely
needed. With the word "behold," which always calls attention to something of more than ordinary importance,
he assures John that there is no cause for him to indulge
in weeping or to give way to despondency, since the
victory has been won. This has been accomplished by
Jesus Christ on the Cross of Calvary, described here in

the graphic words: "the Lion of the tribe of Judah, the
Root of David," of whom dying Jacob long ago had
prophesied (Gen. 49:10) and to whom all the subsequent
Scriptures bear witness (cf. Is. 11:10; Rom. 15:12; Rev.
22:11). The good news here is: The victory has been
achieved by Jesus Christ. He has overcome all enemies
and removed all obstacles and is amply able to reveal and
bring to pass all the prophecies contained in this book.
How fitting it is that the elder as the agent of the Word
should go to the Word itself for a description of this
Victor!

In v. 6 the central feature of this vision, the Vision of
the Lamb, is vividly described. His relation to the throne,
the symbol of authority, power, and rule; His relation to
the four living ones, as the agents of divine providence;
and His relation to the twenty-four elders, are here vividly
portrayed. This Lamb is here described as standing,
i. e., as ready for action (cf. Acts 7:56). Christ as once
slain on the Cross ever remains the One thus slain (1 Cor.
2:2). The Lamb is further described in this verse as
having seven horns and seven eyes. Let us remember
here that the number seven in Revelation always refers
to the relation between God and men. The seven horns
symbolize God's power as directed to the world of men.
The seven eyes are symbols of sight, intelligence, and
wisdom. The expression "which are the seven Spirits of
God" refers, as we have already seen, to the Holy Spirit.
Christ is here represented as having all the power of the
Holy Spirit (cf. 1 Cor. 2:10-11).

In v. 7 is visualized in a dramatic way the act by which
the Lamb came into possession of the book. He "took it
out of the right hand of Him that sat upon the throne,"
i. e., of God. And this He did, not after having previously
asked permission to do so, but as having the right as
Victor to take it (see v. 5). No definite date can be set

for this event; but the fact is frequently expressed in
Scripture (cf. Ps. 110:1; Heb. 1:2-6; Rev. 3:21). In the
next verse the effect of His taking this book is described.
The taking of the book by the Lamb signifies the turning
of its contents into reality in and through the Kingdom
of God. This act brings consternation to God's enemies,
but at the same time calls forth the praises of Christ from
all His agents. Hence the four living ones and the twenty-
four elders are pictured as paying Him homage, just as in
4:10 they are portrayed as paying homage to Him that sat
on the throne, i. e., to God, thus showing that equal worship, honor, and praise are given to the Lamb as to God.
Each one of the twenty-four elders is here pictured as
having harps, or zithers, and golden vials, or bowls, full
of incense odors, which are immediately defined as "the
prayers of saints." The definition explains the symbolism
of the incense bowls, their contents symbolizing the
prayers of the saints, or believers (cf. Ps. 141:2). These
saints, it should be noted, are not glorified saints in
heaven, to whom prayers are never attributed, but saints,
or believers, on earth. It is quite fitting that the Word of
God, of which these elders are the agents, should raise
in them the response of prayers, praise, and thanksgiving.
There is no intimation here of the invocation of the saints.
It is not the twenty-four elders, but the Christians that
are called saints (cf. Rev. 8:3-4; 13:10; 11:18; 18:20).
Nor are these elders conceived of as carrying the prayers
of the saints before the Lamb. Christians do not need
intermediaries to carry their prayers to the Lord.

In vv. 9-10 a record is given of the hymn which these
elders address to the Lamb. Because of its contents it is
called a "new song." The many lambs slain under the
Old Covenant were but types of "the Lamb of God which
taketh away the sin of the world." Now that this Lamb
of God has come and by His sacrificial death has accom-

plished the redemption of man through the shedding of
His blood, the old song of the Old Covenant is transformed into a new song. This calls forth a doxology opening with precisely the same words used in 4:11, where it
is addressed to God. The term "worthy," as also in the
former passage and again in v. 12, carries with it the
meaning of moral worthiness; and the opening of the seals
has the same significance as in vv. 2-5. Why the Lamb is
worthy to execute all that is written in the book and to
turn its prophecies into realities is now explained. The
first thing here recorded is His crucifixion on the Cross of
Calvary, where He shed His precious blood as a ransom
for the sin of the world. The second point recorded indicates the saving effect of the sacrifice He made at so
supreme a price for the redemption of the whole world
of sinners. The mentioning of the objects of Christ's redemption under the four headings, "every kindred and
tongue and people and nation," places strong emphasis on
the universality of Christ's redemption. The communion
of saints surmounts all obstacles.

In v. 10 we have the conclusion of this "new song."
It sets forth the amazing blessings secured by Christ for
the recipients of His kingdom. He has made all believers
"kings," literally, "a kingdom" for our God. Christ as King
establishes His own kingdom — not a kingdom of this
world, but an eternal kingdom that shall never pass
away. Wherever Christ rules with His power and grace,
there He produces His kingdom and constitutes its members heirs of God and joint heirs with Himself, their King.
This kingdom is a unit. All true believers are included
in the one holy Christian Church, which is the communion of saints. These without exception are members
of this one kingdom. But Christ has made them not only
a kingdom, but also "priests." And this applies to every
true Christian, thus bringing out very clearly the spiritual

priesthood of all believers. This new song closes with the
precious promise that all His saints shall reign with Him
on the earth. It is a reigning through serving, as Luther
has it: "That I may live under Him in His kingdom and
serve Him in everlasting righteousness, innocence, and
blessedness, even as He is risen from the dead, lives, and
reigns to all eternity."

In the remaining verses of this chapter John gives expression to what he further saw and heard in this vision
of the throne. He declares that he saw the hosts of angels
and heard what they were saying. These angels John saw
around the throne, i. e., in relation to God's throne, which
here, as everywhere else in Scripture, symbolizes God's
rule, authority, and power. These angels must be clearly
distinguished from the living ones, the agents of God's
providence, and from the elders, the agents of the Word.
The number of these angels, expressed by the multiplica-
tion of myriads by myriads and followed by the multipli-
cation of thousands by thousands, indicates a multitude
beyond all calculation, reminding us of the expression in
Heb. 12:22, "an innumerable company of angels." The
doxology of these angels is introduced here, just as in
4:11, by the word "saying"; and, as is the case in v. 2, this
is done "with a loud voice." The reason for this is that in
both instances it is addressed to the whole universe. This
doxology opens in the same way as in 4:11, but with a
change of person. There it was addressed directly to God.
Here it is ascribed to God and the Lamb. The contents
of the two doxologies are also similar. Only here are
added to the "glory and honor and power" of 4:11 four
more objects, bringing the total number to seven. This
gives expression to their holy completeness, three being
the number of the Deity and four the number of the
world. This means that the universe ascribes these things
to Him as His own possession. Of these ascriptions of

praise the first four are objective, belonging to the Lamb
in His own right, irrespective of all creatures. The last
three are subjective as offered by others to the Lamb.
However, these are not to be separated into so many different objects of praise; but are to be taken together as
constituting a single doxology. Let us not overlook the
fact that here is ascribed to Christ a doxology similar to
that addressed to the Triune God. It was not only the
voices of an innumerable company of angels that John
heard giving glory to God and to the Lamb, but also all
God's creatures throughout the universe. The four places
mentioned (v. 13), heaven, earth, under the earth, and on
the sea, are comprehensive of the whole universe. The
creatures in these four places we certainly cannot enu-
merate; but we should note here that the creatures on
the sea (Greek preposition epí) refer not to creatures in
the depth of the sea, but on its surface; and that the
creatures under the earth refer not to those in Hades, but
to those who had died (cf. Phil. 2:10). What John heard
here was a resumption of the angelic doxology of v. 12
with only a slight reversal in the order and a single change
in the terms, "might" as exercised being substituted for
"strength" as being possessed. In all three doxologies
(4:11; 5:12; 5:13) the ascriptions of praise are enhanced
by connective "ands," thus heaping them up, as it were,
into a tower of praise. To this ascription of praise are
added the words "forever and ever," to show that this
praise is unceasing to all eternity (cf. 1:6).

The last verse in this chapter sets forth the part taken
by the living ones in this doxology. They confirm it by
saying "Amen," i. e., "Yea, yea, it shall be so." In the last
words of this verse is described the part taken by the
elders, the agents of the Word. They are represented
here as falling down in deep devotion and reverent adoration, an act very appropriately climaxing this vision.

Chapter 6

1. And I saw when the Lamb opened one of the seals, and I heard as it were the noise of thunder, one of the four living ones saying: Come and see. 2. And I saw, and, behold, a white horse; and he that sat on him had a bow; and a crown was given unto him; and he went forth conquering and to conquer. 3. And when He had opened the second seal, I heard the second living one say: Come and see. 4. And there went out another horse that was red; and power was given to him that sat thereon to take peace from the earth, and that they should kill one another; and there was given unto him a great sword. 5. And when He had opened the third seal, I heard the third living one say: Come and see. And I beheld, and, lo, a black horse; and he that sat on him had a pair of balances in his hand. 6. And I heard a voice in the midst of the four living ones say: A measure of wheat for a penny, and three measures of barley for a penny; and see thou hurt not the oil and the wine. 7. And when He had opened the fourth seal, I heard the voice of the fourth living one say: Come and see. 8. And I looked, and, behold, a pale horse; and his name that sat on him was Death, and Hell followed with him. And power was given unto them over the fourth part of the earth, to kill with sword, and with hunger, and with death, and with the beasts of the earth. 9. And when He had opened the fifth seal, I saw under the altar the souls of them that were slain for the Word of God and for the testimony which they held; 10. and they cried with a loud voice, saying: How long, O Lord, holy and true, dost Thou not judge and avenge our blood on them that dwell on the earth? 11. And white robes were given unto every one of them; and it was said unto them that they should rest yet for a little season, until their fellow servants also and their brethren that should be killed as they were should be fulfilled. 12. And I beheld when He had opened the sixth seal, and, lo, there was a great earthquake; and the sun became black as sackcloth of hair, and the moon became as blood; 13. and the stars of heaven fell unto the earth, even as a fig tree casteth her untimely figs when she is shaken of a mighty wind. 14. And the heaven departed as a scroll when it is rolled together; and every mountain and island were moved out of their places. 15. And the kings of the earth, and the great men, and the rich

men, and the chief captains, and the mighty men, and every bond-
man, and every free man, hid themselves in the dens and in the
rocks of the mountains; 16. and said to the mountains and rocks:
Fall on us, and hide us from the face of Him that sitteth on the
throne, and from the wrath of the Lamb; 17. for the great day of
His wrath is come; and who shall be able to stand?

---

*B*eginning at Chapter 6 there is recorded the
Vision of the Seven Seals. These seals are
opened successively by the Lamb. John introduces the
opening of the first seal with the words: "And I saw when
the Lamb opened one of the seven seals" (cf. for similar
introduction v. 12). This fixes attention upon the moment
of the first great act, viz., the opening of the first of the
seven seals. Of these seals the first four are closely connected. Each one presents to our view a rider and his
horse, the horse in each case being of a different color.
What John saw when the Lamb opened the first seal is
briefly indicated in v. 2. The same is the case with the
opening of the succeeding seals until the seventh seal is
reached, which, unlike the others, is described at considerable length. This is an indication that this last seal
contains the main revelation, the preceding ones being
subordinate to it. After stating what he saw, John proceeds to tell us what he heard. In each of these four
scenes the horseman is introduced by one of the four
living ones, the agents of God's providential dealing with
men. John declares here that he heard this living one
speaking with a thunderous voice and that the message of
this voice was: "Come." This same message is found at
the opening of each of the first four seals. It was not
addressed to John because he was far off, as some think,
but was addressed to the horseman to bring him into
action, which action immediately follows. In v. 2 John
gives expression to what he saw, introducing it with the

word "behold," to indicate its extreme importance. What
he saw was a white horse and its rider, who with bow
in hand went forth conquering and to conquer. Who this
rider was, we are not told. Various conjectures have been
offered. Some have conjectured that Christ was the rider;
but over against this is the fact that it is Christ the Lamb
who opens the seals, who consequently would hardly
represent Himself as only one of these riders. Others conjecture that the personification here is that of Christianity
in its forward conquering march through the world. But
reference to Matt. 24:14 renders it more probable that it
is the Word of God, the Gospel of the Kingdom, that is
here meant. The horse, being white, symbolizes the holiness of the Word of God. In the statement that this horseman was equipped with a bow, the meaning is simply that
this warrior was prepared for conflict lying before him
and that no enemy can possibly escape the deadly aim of
this weapon. And in the further statement that a crown
was given to him, the meaning is that victory has been
given to this horseman by God, whose Word is victor even
before an arrow has been shot. The use of the two expressions that follow, "conquering and to conquer," emphasizes the conquering career of the Word of God both
in its progressive course and in its finality. This conquering power is directed against the enemies of the Lamb;
and this is the case with all these horsemen (cf. Luther's
battle hymn, stanza 3: "Though devils all the world
should fill, All eager to devour us," etc.).

In v. 3 John describes in words practically identical
with those in v. 1 the Lamb's opening of the second seal.
Here the same message, "Come," calls the second horseman into action. To this horseman riding upon a fiery
red steed, symbolizing war and bloodshed, there was
given power to take peace from the earth; and to this
end a great sword was placed in his hand (cf. Matt. 24:

6-7). This, however, does not refer to any particular wars, but applies to the whole world without restriction. It is not a spiritual conflict that is here described, but real war and bloodshed. Peace being taken from the earth, the slaying of one another begins. The great sword given to this horseman is a merciless weapon, symbol of destruction.

In v. 5 we have a description of the opening of the third seal. It is introduced in words quite similar to those used in the opening of the two preceding seals. What John saw here was a black horse and his rider. The color of this horse corresponds to the image of the horseman and is indicative of a plague, the servant of divine judgment. The black horse and his rider are symbolical of famine. The "pair of balances," more accurately, the "balance," in the hand of this rider, is properly a beam, or bar, uniting the two scales. These scales used for measuring are indicative of scarcity. This is clearly brought out in the next verse. What John here heard was something like a voice. This voice is described as coming from the midst of the four living ones, the agents of God's providence. No speaker is mentioned, all the stress being laid on what this voice says. Like the voice of an auctioneer this voice cries out: "A measure of wheat for a penny, and three measures of barley for a penny." These words are indicative of a prevalent condition of famine (cf. 2 Kings 6:25). And in the expression "hurt not the oil and the wine" a limit is set to this plague of famine ordained by the Lord. The exemption of the oil and the wine is a mitigation of the plague. The Lord God sets bounds to all calamities beyond which they cannot go.

The opening of the fourth seal is described in vv. 7-8. Here John hears the signal for action given to this horseman by the fourth living one in the word "Come."

In v. 8 he tells us what he heard and saw. This time

it was a pale horse and his rider. As in each of these visions, the color of each horse corresponds to the work in which the horseman is engaged. Here the horse is pale, or pallid — a vivid image of death in its most violent and destructive form. Corresponding to this, the name of the rider is definitely stated to be "Death." It is not left to inference as to what his mission was. He is named according to that which he accomplishes, viz., sudden and violent death. The Death-rider slays; and Hades follows after to gather up the souls of those slain. Hades here must not be understood as a generic kingdom, the abode of all souls, believers and unbelievers alike. The souls of believers never enter into Hades at death, but into heaven itself. This is clearly evident from the Parable of Dives and Lazarus (Luke 16:22), also in the case of Stephen (Acts 7:59), and in Paul's case (Phil. 1:23). This rider, as is the case with all these four riders, is a rider of judgment, and as such has nothing to do with the godly. Believers may indeed meet with violent death and with all other forms of calamities; but these are chastisements with which they are visited by God and are evidences of His love for them (cf. John 5:24; 3:18; Heb. 12:5-6). Hades never follows Death to usher the souls of believers into Hades. And the words that follow, "the fourth part of the earth," are not to be understood literally as including all of its inhabitants, believers and unbelievers, but symbolize the extent of the killing, as in 8:7 ff. And the authority mentioned as given to Death and Hades was not given to them by the devil, but by the Lord Himself, whose righteous judgments they are carrying out. The various means by which death is inflicted by them are now noted. The first of these is the sword. The large sword, as the Greek word means, is a fitting emblem of violent destruction. The second means is famine — a torturing, slow, but sure, calamitous death. The third is

death, which here stands for death by pestilence with its
many and overwhelming horrors. The fourth is the beasts
of the earth, i. e., ferocious wild beasts that tear in pieces
and devour their victims in short order.

V. 9 sets forth the opening of the fifth seal. This is a
separate vision and is entirely different from the preceding visions following the opening of each seal. What
John sees here, he sees "in spirit," and not with the natural eye. Since this is so, there is no reason for our asking
the question how John could see souls. Nor is it necessary
to conceive of these souls as clothed in bodies in order
to enable him to see them. The same applies to the position of the souls as "underneath the altar." This expression is purely symbolical, simply indicating their relation
to the sacrificial altar, viz., that the blood of these martyrs
was shed as a holy sacrifice to God and the Lamb. In
a word, the expression shows the true relation in which
the blood of the martyrs stands toward God. In the following verse the souls of these martyrs are represented
as in a conscious state and as crying aloud to God for
vengeance, i. e., for a vindication of His holiness and
justice. In their fervent appeal they address God as absolute Lord and assign to Him the attributes "holy and
true." This is accounted for by the fact that in the slaying
of the martyrs, God's truthfulness, or genuineness, was
impugned and discredited. This cry of theirs is not to be
ascribed to a spirit of vengefulness on their part, as though
it were a call to God to wreak vengeance upon those who
had put them to death. Their appeal to God is rather to
execute His righteous judgment upon the earth dwellers,
i. e., the ungodly, who know and care for nothing beyond
the things of this present world. Their cry has special
reference to the final Judgment, when the day of grace
is ended and only judgment is left. The martyrs who utter
this cry are the Christian martyrs from Stephen, the

prototype, on to the time when John sees this vision. These martyrs had suffered martyrdom for the sake of God's Word and the testimony of Christ; and their cry, "How long?" points to the consummation, which will take place at the end of the world.

In v. 11 is given the answer to the martyrs' question in the preceding verse. First of all, in response to their request and for their assurance, God Almighty gives to each one of them a white robe. This white robe, symbolical of heavenly holiness, is the righteousness of Christ, which is imputed to them and which covers all their sins. The second response to their question is now given. Their good and gracious Lord tells them that they should rest a little while longer until their fellow servants and their brethren, who were about to be killed as they were, should be fulfilled. This is a counsel of patience — a counsel to which we all should give diligent heed whenever troubles, trials, or tribulations confront us in this life. When the full number of believers who follow in the footsteps of these martyrs unto death shall have been gathered in, then the time will be fulfilled, and to each one will be distributed the eternal reward of grace. They are further assured that the period of waiting will not be long: it will be delayed only a little while longer, as God reckons time. Then God's day of wrath will overtake all His enemies, and His holiness and justice will be vindicated to all eternity. What a satisfactory answer to these faithful servants of God!

Now in v. 12 comes the vision of the opening of the sixth seal. Its special significance lies in the fact that it presents a picture of the end — the end of the dispensation of grace and the end of the world as we now know it. This is not here done in full; for other visions to follow place this matter before us again. What this vision gives us are certain features pertaining to the end. These features are in obvious agreement with the immediate signs that will accompany Christ's second coming, as described in Matt. 24:29 and parallel passages. The first feature here mentioned is an earthquake, described as "great" — i. e., not an ordinary earthquake, but an exceedingly violent one. The second feature is the dense blackening of the sun, from which our earth receives its chief light, and the consequent destruction of the light of the moon (cf. Is. 50:3; Joel 2:2; Matt. 24:29). Black is the color of mourning and despair. The reference here is not to any passing eclipse of the sun, but to the blotting out of its light forever. This indicates the close approach of the final Judgment. Further vivid description of this scene is given in v. 13, which graphically depicts the falling of the stars from heaven upon the earth (cf. again Matt. 24:29).

In v. 14 the reactions of the heaven and the earth are described in lurid terms (cf. 2 Peter 3:10; Rev. 16:20). The two last verses of this chapter disclose the effects upon the people of the world of the commotions just described (cf. Christ's own prophecy, Matt. 24:30; Luke 23:30). Six groups or classes of men are here mentioned as overcome with fright and as hiding themselves. The number six is a symbol of the ungodly. The kings mentioned are the chief rulers on earth. The princes are the members of the king's court. The chiliarchs (commanders of a thousand) are the king's generals, or deputies. The rich are men who have great power by reason of their wealth. The strong are those noted for the great influence they exercise on earth. Under the terms "every slave and every free man" are included the whole number of the lower classes of men. All these, overcome by fear and dread, are described as hiding themselves in caves and rocks of the mountains in the vain hope of escaping the wrath of God and of the Lamb, whom they rejected by their unbelief. A striking description of the terrors of the godless on the day of Judgment!

In the next verse we have a graphic description of the terror and dismay of the ungodly, who, finding no protection for themselves in their hiding places, call in gloomy desperation to the mountains and rocks to fall on them and hide them from the face of God and from the wrath of the Lamb, whose grace they have spurned and whose wrath searches them out in the most secret and inaccessible places of the earth. The ground or cause of their terrible despair is definitely stated in the last verse of this chapter. It is because the great day of the wrath of God and the Lamb did come and did overtake them. This calls forth their cry of despair, "Who can stand?" To this rhetorical question there can be but one answer: Not a single one! Only Christians who have by faith appropriated Christ's redemption will lift up their heads in joy because their redemption draweth nigh. For all the ungodly there is no hope, no escape forever and ever. This fact is amply attested in many Scripture passages (cf. Joel 2:2; Mal. 4:1; Nahum 1:6; Matt. 7:22; 1 Cor. 1:8; 1 Thess. 5:2; 2 Pet. 3:10; et al.). Terrible indeed is the vision that John sees on the opening of the sixth seal!

Chapter 7

---

1. *And after these things I saw four angels standing on the four corners of the earth, holding the four winds of the earth, that the wind should not blow on the earth, nor on the sea, nor on any tree. 2. And I saw another angel ascending from the east having the seal of the living God; and he cried with a loud voice to the four angels, to whom it was given to hurt the earth and the sea, 3. saying: Hurt not the earth, neither the sea, nor the trees, till we have*

*sealed the servants of our God in their foreheads. 4. And I heard
the number of them which were sealed; and there were sealed an
hundred and forty and four thousand of all the tribes of the children of Israel. 5. Of the tribe of Juda were sealed twelve thousand. Of the tribe of Reuben were sealed twelve thousand. Of the
tribe of Gad were sealed twelve thousand. 6. Of the tribe of Aser
were sealed twelve thousand. Of the tribe of Nepthalim were
sealed twelve thousand. Of the tribe of Manasses were sealed
twelve thousand. 7. Of the tribe of Simeon were sealed twelve
thousand. Of the tribe of Levi were sealed twelve thousand. Of
the tribe of Issachar were sealed twelve thousand. 8. Of the tribe
of Zabulon were sealed twelve thousand. Of the tribe of Joseph
were sealed twelve thousand. Of the tribe of Benjamin were sealed
twelve thousand. 9. After this I beheld, and, lo, a great multitude,
which no man could number, of all nations and kindreds and
people and tongues, stood before the throne and before the Lamb,
clothed with white robes and palms in their hands; 10. and cried
with a loud voice, saying: Salvation to our God, which sitteth upon
the throne, and unto the Lamb. 11. And all the angels stood round
about the throne and about the elders and the four living ones, and
fell before the throne on their faces and worshiped God, 12. saying:
Amen: Blessing, and glory, and wisdom, and thanksgiving, and
honor, and power, and might be unto our God forever and ever.
Amen. 13. And one of the elders answered, saying unto me: What
are these which are arrayed in white robes? and whence came
they? 14. And I said unto him: Sir, thou knowest. And he said
to me: These are they which came out of great tribulation and
have washed their robes and made them white in the blood of the
Lamb. 15. Therefore are they before the throne of God and serve
Him day and night in His temple; and He that sitteth on the throne
shall dwell among them. 16. They shall hunger no more, neither
thirst any more; neither shall the sun light on them nor any heat.
17. For the Lamb, which is in the midst of the throne, shall feed
them and shall lead them unto living fountains of waters; and God
shall wipe away all tears from their eyes.*

This chapter contains a vision of the Church in
its twofold aspect, the Church Militant and
the Church Triumphant. The Church Militant is treated
in the first eight verses and the Church Triumphant in the

remaining verses of this chapter. This vision is not revealed with the opening of a seal and is in no way connected with the preceding visions. It is not on this account, however, to be regarded as parenthetical or as of minor importance. It is indeed of vital significance for all that follows. The first words of v. 1, "After this," connect what follows with what has just been described in Chapter 6. In this verse John declares that he saw four angels. These were real angels, not imaginary or fictitious angels, but angels of God. He saw these angels standing, i. e., ready for action. The four corners of the earth on which he saw them standing correspond to the four points of the compass and are the starting points from which the four winds proceed. The threefold repetition of the number four in the "four angels, four corners of the earth, and four winds" emphasizes the number of the earth. John further sees these angels as having the four winds of the earth in their control. These winds, as is clear from the context, are not symbolical winds, but actual winds — storms of great violence ready to break loose with great fury from every point of the compass. The purpose for which these four angels are given control of these winds is that they should let them loose upon God's order. They hold the winds in constraint that they may do no damage to earth, sea, or tree till God sees fit for them to accomplish their destructive mission.

In v. 2 John declares that he saw another angel, not an evil angel, but a good angel, an angel of God, as were the other four. He sees this angel coming up from the east and having the seal of the living God. The words "from the east" merely indicate direction. "The seal of the living God" is God's heavenly means for sealing His believing people as His own forever. This angel is next represented as crying with a loud voice to the four angels at the four corners of the earth. As God is in sovereign control of these four angels, it must be conceded that it was He who gave them this commission or authority. From this it follows that this angel, called "another angel," cannot symbolize Christ, as some commentators conjecture on the basis of Mal. 3:1.

V. 3 gives the message to the four angels. It takes the form of a restraining command, prohibiting them from injuring the earth, the sea, and the trees until the work of the sealing angel and his associates is accomplished. This shows that God will permit nothing to interfere with His work in saving His elect. No damage whatever is to be done until all God's faithful servants have been sealed. In the account here given two things should be noted. The first of these is that the sealing is represented as taking place on the forehead of God's servants as the noblest part of their body. The second is that the angel and his associates speak of God as "our God," which is quite appropriate, seeing they have their relation to the same God and are fellow servants of those for whose service they were sent. Sealing is a sign of ownership; and in sealing God acts through agents and means. Hence it is ascribed here to one of God's ministering spirits and to those associated with him. There is no reason for limiting "the servants of God" to Jewish Christians.

In vv. 4-8 John deals with the number of the saved. In v. 4 he declares that he heard the number of those that were sealed — 144,000 of all the tribes of the sons of Israel. He does state that he saw those that were sealed. Later on in 14:1 he declares that he saw and beheld the Lamb standing on Mount Zion, and with Him 144,000 having His name and the name of His Father written on their foreheads. Here he only heard their number — 144,000. This number here is the principal thing. All sorts of interpretations have been placed on this number. The Russellites hold that this is a literal number and claim

that they themselves fill it out. Others limit the number
to Jewish Christians. The fact, however, is that this number is symbolical, being made up of 12×12×1,000. In 4:4
the same two twelves occur, and then are added together
to constitute the 24 elders. Here they are multiplied together, and the sum thus attained is multiplied by the
cube of 10, constituting the number of completeness. The
number thus arrived at symbolizes the complete number
of God's people. This cannot be otherwise, as it is inconceivable that any of God's people are left unsealed.
The expression "sons of Israel" is the name assigned to all
believers (cf. Gen. 32:26-28). The technical name for the
Jewish nation is "Children of Israel." The statement in
vv. 5-8 that 12,000 are sealed out of each tribe, that the
tribe of Dan is omitted from the list, and that the name
of Joseph is substituted for the tribe of Ephraim, is against
the assignment of the number 144,000 to the Jewish
Christians. It also excludes any literal interpretation of
the number. The 12,000 sealed from each tribe are not
represented as being taken out of that particular tribe,
but as completing all of that tribe who were sealed — an
equal number of each tribe. These 144,000 are God's
great nation, an ordered and organized people. And as
being all sealed with the sealing of the servants of God,
they constitute the whole number of the saved. Thus far
is the revelation of the Church Militant. In the succeeding verses follows the Vision of the Church Triumphant.

The expression "After these things" in v. 9 refers to
what has just preceded and marks the advance to what
John now saw. That which John here saw was a multitude so great that it was beyond all calculation. It was
a vision of the Church Triumphant in its state of glory
after all tribulation has forever passed away. This Church
he beholds now after the attainment of its heavenly
blessedness. In speaking of nations and tribes and peoples

and tongues, he indicates the source from which the Church Triumphant was derived; and in describing this multitude as one which no man could number, he stressed the fact that it constitutes the sum total of the saved, a great host gathered from all over the world, the fruit of the Gospel as proclaimed upon earth. This innumerable multitude appears in the vision as standing before the throne and before the Lamb. The throne, as we have previously noted, is the symbol of God's eternal power, rule, and dominion. The Lamb, before whom they stand, is Jesus Christ, the Savior, who purchased them with the stupendous sacrifice of His precious blood. The white robes with which all in this vast multitude are clothed are symbolical here as elsewhere of holiness. The palms in their hands symbolize triumphant victory over all foes. In the verse immediately following John describes to us the cry which these blessed saints, now in eternal glory, utter. With a loud voice they give vent to hymns of praise to God, who is the Author of their complete and perfected salvation, and to the Lamb, the Mediator of their salvation, by whose atoning sacrifice they have been delivered from sin and death and every evil; and translated into His presence, they now and evermore enjoy the beatific vision of God. How could it be otherwise than that such situation should call forth their loudest and profoundest praise!

In vv. 11-12 John vividly describes the effect this had upon the angels, God's "ministering spirits sent forth to minister for them who shall be heirs of salvation." Now that this has been accomplished, all God's angels, an innumerable host (v. 11), standing round about the throne and about the elders and the four living ones, "fell down before the throne upon their faces and worshiped God." In confirmation of the praise given to God by the Church as recorded in v. 10, they also ascribe praise to God for.

the salvation which He has accomplished for sinful men. Their ascription begins and closes with "Amen, yea, yea, it shall be so," as a word of confirmation, thus giving their approval of the praise rendered by the Church Triumphant. As divine power and might are exhibited in the deliverance of mankind, it is only natural that thanksgiving and honor and glory should be given to God not only by the glorified believers themselves, but also by the multitude of the heavenly host (v. 11). The appearance of the great multitude of white-robed saints suggested a question. To this one of the agents of God's Word gave answer with a twofold question — a question not dealing with their number, but with their origin and character. The marvel here is that so great a multitude of sinners should appear in white robes of heavenly holiness. How did this happen?

In v. 14 John answers this question of one of the elders. Addressing him reverently as "my Lord," John puts it up to the living one to reveal what the vision was intended to impart in the words "thou knowest." The answer is at once forthcoming and is recorded for our edification in the remaining words of this verse to the end of this chapter. First of all, he tells John that these are they that came out of great tribulation. This "great tribulation" is frequently misinterpreted especially by Millennialists, who take this as referring to the great tribulation at the end of the world just previous to Christ's second coming. Against this is the fact, that this would not affect the whole Church, but only those actually living in the last days. The "great tribulation" here is to be understood as comprehending all tribulations through which the Church of true believers passes previous to its entrance into the Kingdom of Glory. No other interpretation would cover the whole Church from the beginning to the end of time. In this vision John sees the Church in its glorified state, all tribulation being a thing of the past, and no more tribulation remaining. Nothing henceforth to all eternity shall harm these holy saints of God. Secondly, he informs John that these saints have washed their robes and made them white in the blood of the Lamb. This describes a single act, whitening by washing their robes in the blood of the Lamb. The picture is thus rendered all the more vivid and strikingly presents the cleansing power of Christ's blood (cf. Heb. 9:14; 1 John 1:7-9). All true Christians who put their trust in the blood atonement of Jesus Christ, the Lamb of God, have their robes washed and made white in the blood of the Lamb. No act of their own is ascribed to them, and no merit is claimed by them. All their blessedness in the Kingdom of Glory is due not to themselves, but to the bloody sacrifice of Jesus Christ on the Cross of Calvary and to His perfectly holy life, both of which are imputed to them without any merit, or deserving, on their part. In the two remaining verses of this chapter the blessedness of the saints in glory is described, both negatively and positively. Hunger and thirst are the cause of much distress in this world; and the smiting of the sun and every other form of heat occasion much suffering. These things, mentioned because of their intensity, symbolize all the hardships, pains, and afflictions that come upon believers in this world. In the Church Triumphant all these sufferings are forever done away, and none of them to all eternity shall afflict the saints any more (cf. 21:4; Is. 25:8).

In the next verse, on the positive side, it is explained why this is so. The reason is that the Lamb of God, exalted and sitting upon the throne of glory at God's right hand, shall shepherd them. This He can and will do, because as their Good Shepherd upon earth He gave His life for the sheep and made them His flock. Furthermore,

He will also lead them to fountains of waters of life. The Lord who came into the world that men "might have life, and that they might have it more abundantly," is pictured here as leading the glorified saints to life's springs of waters. This living water He will supply to them unceasingly and abundantly to all eternity. All the saved are dependent upon Him for their blessed life. And in the final statement, "and God shall wipe away all tears from their eyes," there is given the comforting assurance that no tear shall ever mar the eternal, abiding joy of the saints in heaven.

Chapter 8

1. And when he had opened the seventh seal, there was silence in heaven about the space of half an hour. 2. And I saw the seven angels which stood before God; and to them were given seven trumpets. 3. And another angel came and stood at the altar having a golden censer; and there was given unto him much incense that he should offer it with the prayers of all saints upon the golden altar which was before the throne. 4. And the smoke of the incense which came with the prayers of the saints ascended up before God out of the angel's hand. 5. And the angel took the censer and filled it with fire of the altar and cast it into the earth; and there were voices and thunderings and lightnings and an earthquake. 6. And the seven angels which had the seven trumpets prepared themselves to sound. 7. The first angel sounded, and there followed hail and fire mingled with blood, and they were cast upon the earth; and the third part of trees was burnt up, and all green grass was burnt up. 8. And the second angel sounded, and as it were a great mountain burning with fire was cast into the sea; and the third part of the sea became blood; 9. and the third part of the creatures which were in the sea, and had life, died; and the third part of the ships were destroyed. 10. And the third angel sounded,

and there fell a great star from heaven, burning as it were a lamp,
and it fell upon the third part of the rivers and upon the fountains
of waters; 11. and the name of the star is called Wormwood: and
the third part of the waters became wormwood; and many men
died of the waters because they were made bitter. 12. And the
fourth angel sounded, and the third part of the sun was smitten
and the third part of the moon and the third part of the stars, so as
the third part of them was darkened, and the day shone not for a
third part of it, and the night likewise. 13. And I beheld, and heard
an angel flying through the midst of heaven, saying with a loud
voice: Woe, woe, woe, to the inhabiters of the earth by reason of
the other voices of the trumpet of the three angels which are yet
to sound!

This chapter begins with the opening of the seventh seal, described in practically the same words as in the description of the opening of the preceding seals. The immediate consequence of the opening of this seventh and last seal was that it was followed by silence in heaven for about half an hour. This impressive silence in heaven, where the praises of God and the Lamb resounded, as described in the preceding chapter, may be interpreted as a silence of awe and expectancy as to what is to follow upon the opening of this seal because of its peculiar contents. That this silence lasted for about a half hour describes the impression made upon John. It is a silence in which all voices are hushed and which ushers in the seven trumpet judgments and the seven bowls of the wrath of God and of the plagues that follow. In v. 2 the same formula is used by which John indicated what the seals previously opened enabled him to see. Here he saw seven angels standing before God. There is nothing to indicate that these seven angels were archangels, or angels of high rank constituting a hierarchy; but they are described merely as angels standing in close relation to God, angels whom He has selected to give the signals for

His impending judgments. The number seven is symbolical as containing the number three as referring to God and the number four as referring to the world with which He is about to reckon. For the purpose of executing their task there were given to them seven trumpets. The significance of these trumpets stands out in striking contrast to that of the seals. Seals hide and conceal: trumpets signal and announce.

In v. 3 another angel is introduced as standing at the altar with a golden censer, to whom much incense was given. While it is not definitely stated here by whom this was done, the implication is that it was by God Himself, whose ministering servant this angel, like all the other angels, is. The purpose clause, which now follows, shows why much incense was given to this angel. It was that he might offer it up with the prayers of all the saints. This angel is represented as ministering at the altar of incense, offering upon it the incense with the prayers of all the saints. From the altar of incense the prayers of the saints are already ascending like the smoke of incense to God before the throne, which is the symbol of God's eternal dominion, rule, and power. The implication is that these prayers and this incense are acceptable to God. The incense smoke going up to God out of the angel's hands for the prayers of the saints symbolizes Christ's special intercession for His believing people, adding power and efficacy to their prayers. The Lord thus interceding for His people renders their prayers addressed to God in His name all the more acceptable. To these prayers of the saints the angel in this vision contributes nothing. He makes no intercession and offers no prayer of his own, but merely gives to their prayers the incense given to him for this purpose. The prayers here mentioned are not limited as to either content or source. All worship is here included in these prayers, such as peti-

tions, thanksgiving, praise, etc. And under the term
"saints" all true believers on earth from the first to the
last are included. We must remember that with God all
time is an eternal now.

In v. 5 there is given a lively description of the act
of this angel. The angel took the censer, filled it from
the fire of the altar, and then hurled the fire from the
censer to the earth, thus representing the divine answer
to the prayers of the saints as accompanied by the intercession of Christ. The consequence following the hurling
of the fire from the censer to the earth by the angel is
described as "voices and thunderings and lightnings and
an earthquake." All these fearful things are preparatory
to the introduction of the trumpet angels and their action
in sounding their trumpets of judgment. All these words,
which occur again in 11:19 with the addition of "great
hail," and again in 16:18, where the earthquake is described as "great," are manifestations of God's power and
dominion; and it is useless to attempt to give separate
interpretation to each.

V. 6 now gives us an impressive introduction to the
action of the seven trumpet angels, whose sounding of
the trumpet is successively describ d together with the
results that follow. All that has been said in the preceding verses of this chapter forms the ground for these
trumpet judgments. Much allegorizing has been indulged
in by commentators about these seven trumpets; but, as
this is due largely to imagination, it carries with it no
convincing proof. The only clear point here is, that these
trumpets exhibit world-wide, miraculous judgments and
that the first six reach their climax in the seventh.

In v. 7 the first angel is pictured as sounding the
trumpet; and the consequences that immediately followed are vividly described as the coming of hail and
fire mixed with blood. This excludes the interpretation

of this hail and fire mixed with blood as being a natural
thing. Of these it is further said that they were cast to
the earth. By whom this was done is not stated in so
many words; but as this judgment is God's, it is evident
that this is the work of His hand. The terrible effects of
the casting of this blood-mingled hail and fire to the
earth are described as the burning up of a third of the
trees and of all green grass. This effect is supernatural;
and all allegorizing attempts to apply this to historical, or
particular calamities are vain speculations. The supernatural features simply serve to heighten the effect. The
chief thing here is the effect produced. The more terrible
the effect, the more terrible is the supernatural cause.
The plagues in Exodus 7 ff. furnish to some extent a
parallel; but those of the trumpets far surpass them in
their terribleness. In both cases the plagues are supernatural disasters. The Egyptian plagues affected all
Egypt. These here recorded affect the whole world.
Physical features are used only to make the matter visible
to the eyes of John. The best explanation of the four
trumpet blasts described in this chapter is, that they are
religious delusions sent by God in punishment of those
who take pleasure in unrighteousness and will not receive
the truth of the Gospel unto their salvation (cf. 2 Thess.
2:11-12). God's patience and long-suffering having
reached its limit, destructive delusions are sent upon
those who loved the ways of unrighteousness and found
their pleasure therein. These judgments are presented in
four stages, each one surpassing its predecessor in severity. In this first trumpet vision the destructive power is
strongly emphasized by the thrice-repeated verb "burned
up"; but that the devastation was not total is brought out
by the statement, that this applies only to a third part of
the earth and its trees. And yet how horrible is this de-

lusion even in its first stage! It is as though only utter devastation were left in its wake.

In vv. 8-9 there stands recorded the second trumpet judgment. This bears some resemblance to the second Egyptian plague, the turning of the waters into blood, but far surpasses it in terror and destructive power. This judgment advances over the preceding one in that to the judgment upon the land, judgment upon the sea is added. The scene depicted here, just as in the case of the first trumpet judgment, is supernatural. In this ghastly picture there is given a scene of vast destructiveness — the continued destructive power of religious delusions portrayed in the preceding trumpet blast. Here likewise the destruction is not complete, only a third being turned into blood, or dying, or being destroyed.

In the next two verses we have an account of the sounding of the third trumpet judgment. This marks an advance over the damage inflicted at the blast of the trumpet by the second angel and denotes something quite different from it. These preparatory visitations are presented in such a way that one blow follows upon another until the end is reached. Here we have the picture of a great star from heaven burning like a torch and falling upon the third part of the rivers and upon the fountains of waters. All these expressions designate it as something supernatural. The main point here is again the frightful damage, or ruinous effect, which the falling of this star has. The context shows that the effect is none other than that which has been determined by the will of God. Conclusive proof that this was no natural star is that so great a star falling upon the earth is limited in its damage to only a third part of its rivers and its fountains of waters. The name of this star, Wormwood, literally, Absinthe, also does not agree with any star known to men. This affords further proof that it is no natural star, or comet,

or other phenomenon, that is here described; but that the
name is a part of the symbolism characterizing this narrative. The effect of the falling of this star upon the rivers
and fountains of waters, together with the disaster it
brought to men, is now distinctly described. It made the
waters bitter; and the result was that it brought death to
many of the people who had nothing else to drink. This
third trumpet judgment advances over the preceding ones
in its description of the terrible judgment which comes
upon the world because of its religious delusion on account of its rejection of the Gospel, which should reign
supreme in all the avenues of life. To imbibe wormwood
instead of the sweetness of the Gospel is something awful.
May it not be our experience!

V. 12 places before us the fourth trumpet judgment —
the smiting of the third part of each of the three heavenly
bodies, sun, moon, and stars. That this resulted in the
darkening of the third of the day and of the third of the
night, clearly demonstrates the supernatural nature of this
judgment. This judgment, like the preceding ones, deals
with religious delusion and carries still further the idea
of destructiveness. "Terrible is the judgment when the
light of the Word is taken away in any degree." Lenski.
The darkening in this fourth trumpet vision is nothing
else than a darkening of the Word of God. This is referred to in Amos 8:11-12 as "a famine of hearing the
words of the Lord"; and in Matt. 13:13-15 the Lord Himself refers to it as a hiding of the truth in judgment upon
those who had hardened their hearts and closed their ears
to God's holy Word. Is this not indeed a mighty call to us
to be on our guard?

V. 13 is preparatory for the three trumpet judgments
that are yet to be sounded. The term "angel" (A. V.) in
this verse should, according to the best Greek manuscripts, be changed to "eagle." This eagle John saw flying

in midheaven, where it may be seen and where its voice may be heard by all to whom its message is directed. With a loud voice this eagle, referring to the three trumpets that are yet to sound, gives an intimation of the serious character of the judgments that they will usher in and pronounces three woes upon all the earth dwellers for their rejection of the gracious Gospel of life and salvation. While these words were directly addressed to John, they are words which we all would do well to take to heart. The sounding of the remaining trumpet judgments will be terrible far beyond the preceding ones, each succeeding one increasing over its predecessor in its drastic nature (cf. 9:12; 11:14). Here again there is no ground for allegorizing.

Chapter 9

1. *And the fifth angel sounded, and I saw a star fall from heaven unto the earth; and to him was given the key of the bottomless pit. 2. And he opened the bottomless pit; and there arose a smoke out of the pit as the smoke of a great furnace; and the sun and the air were darkened by reason of the smoke of the pit. 3. And there came out of the smoke locusts upon the earth; and unto them was given power as the scorpions of the earth have power. 4. And it was commanded them that they should not hurt the grass of the earth, neither any green thing, neither any tree, but only those men which have not the seal of God in their foreheads. 5. And to them it was given that they should not kill them, but that they should be tormented five months; and their torment was as the torment of a scorpion when he striketh a man. 6. And in those days shall men seek death, and shall not find it; and shall desire to die, and death shall flee from them. 7. And the shapes of the locusts were like unto horses prepared unto battle; and on their heads were as it were crowns like gold, and their faces were as the faces of men.*

8. *And they had hair as the hair of women, and their teeth were as the teeth of lions.* 9. *And they had breastplates, as it were breastplates of iron; and the sound of their wings was as the sound of chariots of many horses running to battle.* 10. *And they had tails like unto scorpions, and there were stings in their tails; and their power was to hurt men five months.* 11. *And they had a king over them, which is the angel of the bottomless pit, whose name in the Hebrew tongue is Abaddon, but in the Greek tongue hath his name Apollyon.* 12. *One woe is past; and, behold, there come two woes more hereafter.* 13. *And the sixth angel sounded, and I heard a voice from the four horns of the golden altar which is before God,* 14. *saying to the sixth angel which had the trumpet: Loose the four angels which are bound in the great river Euphrates.* 15. *And the four angels were loosed, which were prepared for an hour and a day and a month and a year for to slay the third part of men.* 16. *And the number of the army of the horsemen were two hundred thousand thousand; and I heard the number of them.* 17. *And thus I saw the horses in the vision, and them that sat on them, having breastplates of fire and of jacinth and brimstone; and the heads of the horses were as the heads of lions; and out of their mouths issued fire and smoke and brimstone.* 18. *By these three was the third part of men killed, by the fire and by the smoke and by the brimstone which issued out of their mouths.* 19. *For their power is in their mouth and in their tails; for their tails were like unto serpents, and had heads, and with them they do hurt.* 20. *And the rest of the men which were not killed by these plagues, yet repented not of the works of their hands, that they should not worship devils, and idols of gold, and silver, and brass, and stone, and of wood, which neither can see nor hear nor walk;* 21. *neither repented they of their murders nor of their sorceries nor of their fornication nor of their thefts.*

---

*T*his chapter, which introduces the fifth and sixth trumpet blasts, presents judgments of a far more terrible nature than any, or all that have preceded them. The judgments here described are direct supernatural inflictions from God. Being judgments upon those who in their deadly delusion willfully reject God's truth, they strike so intensely that they can be pictured

adequately only by that which is unnatural and monstrous. These two judgments advance progressively: the
fifth exhibiting the hellish delusion in its tormenting effects, the sixth in its killing effects. All the delusions
pictured in these visions as spreading woe, torment, and
death over the ungodly earth dwellers, are religious delusions. From their source these delusions spread far and
wide and are found wherever the Gospel is rejected. We
are living among many of them today.

In v. 1 John describes what he saw upon the sounding
of the trumpet by the fifth angel. This was a star that
had fallen out of heaven to the earth, to which was given
the key of the bottomless pit. The star here mentioned
is no physical star, but a personification. This is evident
from the fact that to this star was given the key of the
pit of the abyss and that with this key he opened it. This
also excludes the designation of the star as Satan, since
he neither fell out of heaven to the earth nor holds a key
with which to open the abyss. The statement here simply
places the star where it is in position to open the abyss.
The personification of the star represents this judgment
as coming from God as a curse upon men. Many commentators conceive of the abyss as the realm of the dead;
but the fact cannot be denied that this word as used in
Revelation designates only the present abode of the devil
and his angels; and the key which was given to this star
was for the purpose of opening the pit of the abyss which
was locked. This power to open the pit of hell and allow
its infernal punitive powers of delusion to burst forth
upon the earth is a divine, not a devilish power (cf.
Christ's own words in 1:18).

In v. 2 down to v. 11 inclusive we have a description
of the opening of the pit by the star with the key that
had been given to him and the startling effects that en-
sued. He opened the pit, which presumably had been

covered, in order that that which was within might emerge. Immediately upon its opening there arose smoke like the smoke of a mighty furnace. The result of its issuing from the mouth of the pit is vividly described as the darkening of the light of the sun and the spreading of its pall over the very air that men breathe. This is a figurative picture of the blotting out of the light of truth from men's minds and a darkening of their understanding and all their thinking. This hellish curse is sent by God upon men because of their persistent neglect of His Word of truth, which alone could save them. In the second verse a vast increase in the evil is described. Not only was all light blotted out, but out of this smoke came forth a dreadful swarm of hellish locusts to put into execution the plagues which were assigned to them. These locusts, of course, are not to be taken literally. There were never any locusts like these on the earth. They transcend our wildest imagination. To them was given power, i. e., by God, for the carrying out of their task. This power is likened to that of earthly scorpions, because of the terrific pain inflicted. Such horrible imagery is used to convey some idea of the hellish curse that is sent upon the earth and to give an inkling of its terribleness.

In the fourth verse a limit is set by God to the tormenting and destructive power of these creatures. By His express command true believers, those who have received His seal, are exempted from the judgments which these infernal locusts execute. But all who have not this seal will, without a single exception, meet this affliction. By God's own command, no harm is allowed to be inflicted by these hellish delusions upon any of those who are His by faith. They will strike all despisers of God's Word, but leave true believers unscathed. What a precious treasure we Christians have here in God's protecting

providence! God also limits the destructive power of
these diabolical creatures over their victims. This is
brought out in v. 5, where, though their torment is likened
to the torment of a scorpion, when it striketh a man, it is
definitely stated that they were not permitted to kill
them, but only to torment them. Their torment, however,
far from being mild, was inconceivably severe. Untold
myriads of these locust monsters strike their victims with
myriads of horrible things. This torment of their victims,
it is declared, was to continue for five months. This
number is certainly not to be taken literally; neither is it
to be taken as year-months or mystical days; but is to be
explained from the figure ten, which is the symbol of
completeness. Since their torment does not kill, it is,
therefore, not complete. So terrible will it be that the
victims will seek death but will not find it. They will
want to die, but death will flee from them. This stage of
torment presents a curse upon delusion that is beyond
calculation and drives its victims into the very depth of
despair. But, thanks be to God! from its evil effects all
believers in the Word, who have the peace of God in their
hearts, are delivered.

In vv. 7-10 we have a description of these locusts in
seven aspects or features, which characterize them. The
whole description is unnatural, actually monstrous; but it
accurately describes the terrible delusion here symbolized, the effects of which are experienced by all who have
not the seal of God upon them. The first feature in the
description of these horrible locusts is their likeness in
shape to horses prepared for battle. This imagery is, of
course, contrary to all nature. No natural locusts ever
presented such an appearance. The idea here to be conveyed is their terrifying effect — "like horses fitted for
battle." The second feature represents them as wearing
on their heads "crowns like gold." These golden crowns

are symbolical of victory, implying that there is no possibility of withstanding them or of escaping from them.
This delusion is a judgment curse of the most terrifying
nature upon all the unbelieving and ungodly. The third
feature describes them as having faces like the faces of
human beings. This is anomalous, as no locust ever had
such a face; but it designates them as having human intelligence far transcending all animal instinct. Thus is
this brood of hell distinguished from all the products of
earth, or of nature, or of human wickedness.

V. 8. The fourth feature of these locusts is that their
hair is as the hair of women. This follows naturally upon
the description of them as having faces of human beings,
and also clearly shows that they were not natural, but
supernatural locusts. The fifth feature pictures them as
having teeth as the teeth of lions. This does not indicate
their voraciousness; for later on (v. 10) we are told that
their power to do damage is in their tails and that even
with these they do not kill. Here we have only another
concrete and visible representation of their power for the
infliction of evil, from which there is no shelter apart from
that afforded by the Word of God.

The sixth feature is described in v. 9. Here they are
pictured as fully equipped for war, having breastplates
of iron and rushing in innumerable chariots into battle,
thus overwhelming everything that lies in their path. To
this is added that the sound of their wings was as the
sound of many horses running to battle. What a ghastly
description here of this terrible delusion, which destroys
everything in its wake!

In v. 10 the seventh feature of these locusts is described. They are pictured here as having tails like the
tails of scorpions, which, of course, is not the case with
natural locusts. This has special significance, because
their power to hurt human beings lies in their tails in

which their stings reside. This is an indication of their
malicious force. They do not, however, kill their victims,
but torment them most grievously. That their power to
hurt men was for five months indicates no definite length
of time, the number five here, as in v. 5, being a number
symbolizing incompleteness.

In v. 12 is described the fifth type of delusion which
these locusts inflict upon men. These demoniacal locusts,
unlike natural locusts, are represented as having a king
over them. This king is further described as the angel of
the abyss. This does not mean Satan, or an angel appointed by him as overseer of the abyss, or as the star
mentioned in v. 1. The angel of the abyss, as the king of
the locusts over which he reigns, exists only in the vision
and cannot be more concisely interpreted. The names
"Abaddon" and "Apollyon" are symbolical and denote
perdition. They are assigned to this angel to characterize
the type of delusion which these locusts inflict upon men.
It is a delusion ascending out of the abyss that inevitably
leads to perdition. Let us ever be on our guard against
so frightful a calamity!

V. 12 concludes the report of this fifth trumpet judgment that has now passed out of John's sight and points
to two woes yet to come.

In v. 13 the blast of the trumpet by the sixth angel is
introduced in precisely the same way as was the case
with the blasting of the trumpet by the preceding angels.
The judgment curse which follows is also similar but
exceeds them in its frightfulness. This woe likewise comes
from God and is sent by Him as a curse. It is a serious
mistake to conceive of this woe as a natural one and to
assign it to wars in general, or to the invasion of the
Mohammedans, which resulted in the fall of Constanti-
nople, as is done by some commentators. This, like all
the others, is not a natural phenomenon, but a super-

natural judgment in the form of delusion that proceeds
out of hell itself. The fact that John heard this voice
coming from the golden altar which is before God, indicates this woe as being a curse or judgment coming
directly from God. That John heard this voice from the
four horns indicates that it proceeded from the center of
the altar table where the incense burns, whence (8:3)
the prayers of the saints with the accompanying incense
ascend up to God.

In v. 14 is given the message which the voice from the
four horns of the golden altar addresses to the sixth
angel. It is an order to set free the four angels that were
bound at the great river Euphrates. These angels are not
to be identified with the four angels of 7:1; still less are
they to be reckoned as evil angels. The fact that these
angels are described as being bound indicates only that
hitherto they have been held in check. The time has
now arrived that they should be loosed to execute the
judgments with which they are charged. The river
Euphrates does not indicate a geographical location, but
is mentioned because of its connection with the great
world powers of Assyria, Babylon, and Persia, whose
dominion extended over the then-known world with
devastating power. The great river Euphrates symbolizes
world dominance. The immediate consequence of the
angel's obedience to the order given to him is set forth
in v. 14. The four angels were loosed to carry out the
judgment with which they were charged. These angels,
it is further stated, were prepared, manifestly by God,
whose ministering spirits they are, for a definite time, the
date of which is known only to God, who holds the times
and the seasons in His own power. The purpose for which
they were loosed was that they might kill the third of
human beings. This shows an advance over the destructive powers described in Chapter 7; and the fraction one

third, here as there, shows that the judgment is not complete, but will be followed by others still more terrible.

In v. 16 the number of these horsemen is given, agreeing quite closely with the enumeration in 5:11, but having no actual connection with it. This immense number, 200,000,000, cannot possibly be taken, as is done by many commentators, to denote the armies of the Saracens, since the armies here are made up of horsemen, and no mention is made of artillery, which the Mohammedans employed in their warfare. The only significance in this vast number is that it is more than sufficient to effect the killing on which it was bent.

In the following verse John tells how he came by the knowledge of the overwhelming number of these horsemen. The number was revealed to him, and he heard it. Now he sees them in the vision and proceeds to describe them in detail. His description of the equipment of these riders is a designation of the three hellish colors, fiery, dark red, and yellow — a description drawn from the pictures of hell itself frequently found in this book (cf. 14: 10-11; 19:20; 20:10). This description adds vastly to the horrors of the scene. Immediately after this he proceeds to describe the horses on which these riders sat. His frightful description of them as having heads like lions shows conclusively that this is a description not of natural, but of supernatural horses. His further description of these horses as breathing out fire and smoke and brimstone increases the frightful sense of horror that they inspire.

The effects of these three plagues are vividly described in v. 18. In the preceding fifth plague the locusts tormented but did not kill the third of human beings. Here these armies do not simply torment, but actually kill the third of the human race by means of these three plagues, smoke, fire, and brimstone. The hellish effects of horror and death are ascribed to these horsemen.

In v. 19 an explanation is given of the killing of the third of human beings by these horses. It is pointed out that the power to kill resides in the mouth of these horses. It is definitely stated that it is only the horses that kill. Nothing at all is said of their riders or of any weapons with which they are equipped. Only the colors of these riders correspond to the fire, smoke, and brimstone coming out of the mouth of these millions of horses. It is further pointed out that power also resides in their tails, which are here described as like unto serpents. They kill with what issues from their mouths, but only hurt with their tails. This indicates a second and minor curse inflicted by these horses. Neither the horses nor their riders resemble any cavalry force on earth. Hence it is a glaring mistake when commentators apply this picture to the armies of the Turks or to any other armies. Like all the trumpet woes, it applies only to the curse of hellish delusion, which overruns the world and prevents it from becoming Christian. This is manifest in the rapid widespreading of such delusions as atheism, materialism, false philosophy, false science, negative criticism, faulty morality, and heresies of all kinds, which kill the spiritual life of people all over the world in ever-increasing numbers.

In the last two verses of this chapter is given a description of the unbelievers or earth dwellers who were not killed by the six plagues just described. Notwithstanding the severity of all these curse judgments, especially of the last, these wicked people did not amend their evil ways, or experience any change of heart, but were all the more stiffened in their resistance of God's holy will and hardened in their impenitence. They constantly continued in their sinful courses and forsook not the works

of their hands. An enumeration is now given of their evil
works which they continued so eagerly to pursue. This
worship of devils and dumb idols of every description is
a picture of the gravest paganism; at the same time it is
a picture of the effect of spiritual delusions upon men.
They will revert to image worship and gross idolatry,
from which all the culture in the world will not save them
apart from the Gospel of Jesus Christ, the only Gospel of
our salvation (1 Cor. 10:20). Of these images it is declared that they are powerless things, unable either to
see or hear or walk. Included here — let us not forget it —
are all sins against the First Commandment, such as the
false gods of pagans, Jews, Mohammedans, materialists,
pseudo scientists, evolutionists, Mormons, Russellites,
Swedenborgians, etc. Although the holy Gospel has now
been preached for many centuries, it still finds these
fanatics not only impenitent, but eager and zealous in the
spreading of their pernicious propaganda throughout the
world. The sins described in this verse are committed
directly against God.

In the next verse follows a description of the sins of
these earth dwellers against the Second Table of the
Law. The first of these is murder, including all sins
against the Fifth Commandment; and closely connected
with it sorceries — devilish spells cast upon men to their
hurt. Next come fornications, sins against the Sixth Commandment. And let us remember here that, while these
sins are widely prevalent in heathendom, sexual vices are
found in ever-increasing measure even among the so-
called Christian nations of our day. Finally are mentioned
sins against the Seventh Commandment, sins that are
prevalent not only in heathen lands, but everywhere
throughout the whole world.

No repentance is found for any, or all these sins,
among the earth dwellers who escaped the previous woes.

They are only strengthened in their impenitence and the more determined to continue in their desperately wicked courses. Can we really say that the world is any better today? The time has now arrived for the blast of the last trumpet ushering in the final Judgment.

Chapter 10

1. *And I saw another mighty angel come down from heaven, clothed with a cloud; and a rainbow was upon his head, and his face was as it were the sun, and his feet as pillars of fire; 2. and he had in his hand a little book open; and he set his right foot upon the sea and his left foot on the earth, 3. and cried with a loud voice as when a lion roareth; and when he had cried, seven thunders uttered their voices. 4. And when the seven thunders had uttered their voices, I was about to write; and I heard a voice from heaven saying unto me: Seal up those things which the seven thunders uttered, and write them not. 5. And the angel which I saw stand upon the sea and upon the earth lifted up his hand to heaven, 6. and sware by Him that liveth forever and ever, who created heaven, and the things that therein are, and the earth, and the things that therein are, and the sea, and the things which are therein, that there should be time no longer; 7. but in the days of the voice of the seventh angel, when he shall begin to sound, the mystery of God should be finished, as He hath declared to His servants, the prophets. 8. And the voice which I heard from heaven spake unto me again and said: Go and take the little book which is open in the hand of the angel which standeth upon the sea and upon the earth. 9. And I went unto the angel and said unto him: Give me the little book. And he said unto me: Take it and eat it up; and it shall make thy belly bitter, but it shall be in thy mouth sweet as honey. 10. And I took the little book out of the angel's hand and ate it up; and it was in my mouth sweet as honey; and as soon as I had eaten it, my belly was bitter. 11. And he said unto me: Thou must prophesy again before many peoples and nations and tongues and kings.*

*J*ust as between the opening of the sixth and seventh seals a vision of the Church in its militant and triumphant state appears, so now between the sounding of the sixth and the seventh trumpet a vision of the Church again appears to John, combined with the witness of the Word. In each case the vision of the Church stands in essential connection with the preceding visions and sheds light upon them (see Chapters 7 and 10). The six trumpet judgments did not affect the Church, but were curses of judgment upon the deluded world separated from God and His Kingdom of Grace. The present vision is a separate one and is not to be confused with the sixth trumpet judgment or connected with it in any chronological way. All these judgment visions are worldwide in their scope and are sent upon the nations because of their refusal to give heed to the precious message of the glorious Gospel of Jesus Christ, the only Gospel of salvation.

In v. 1 John describes his vision of another angel in words precisely the same as in 8:3 except for the addition of the word "strong." This precludes the conception of this angel as representing Christ, as is done by many commentators. While certain features of this angel, as, e. g., his face and feet, remind us of the description of Christ in 1:15-16, the term "angel" as here used in the Apocalypse cannot here be applied to Christ, as no angel can ever equal Christ. This angel is here called "strong" because of his whole appearance and because of the action ascribed to him. John saw this angel coming down out of heaven. Remembering that this is a vision and that John was "in the spirit," we need not worry ourselves that John, who in 4:1 presumably was in heaven, now apparently is on earth; nor need we puzzle ourselves as to how he went from one place to the other. The vision is sufficient in itself, and it is idle to indulge in speculations about it. John describes this angel further as having a cloud thrown round about him and as having a rainbow upon his head. This description is a striking reminder of God's gracious covenant made with mankind after the Flood, and of which the rainbow in the cloud was the sign. The appearance of this angel thus arrayed is an assurance to the congregation of believers of their separation from the antichristian world religion, and also of their safety under the protection of Almighty God, who, in the midst of His severest judgments upon the ungodly, remains ever faithful to His eternal covenant of grace with His believing children. This rainbow upon the head of the angel as God's messenger, is a symbol of peace — the peace of God that is brought to the congregation of believers. The description of the face of this angel as similar to the sun and of his feet as being like pillars of fire is an indication of his glory and of his power — a power of such a nature as to inspire terror. In v. 2 this glorious angel is described as holding a little book open in his hand. This stands in sharp contrast with the book mentioned in 5:1 ff. There it was God's large book of judgments closed and sealed, and not to be opened until all God's judgment strokes have reached their goal. This book contained the most powerful and profound secrets of eternity. The present book, on the other hand, is a small book and open, and is offered not only to the Church, or congregation of all believers, but to the whole world. The posture of this angel with his feet spreading over the whole world has also to do with this little book, on which everything in this vision culminates and centers (cf. v. 11). Note the enormous proportions of this angel, his head high enough to be clothed with a cloud and his feet extending from ocean to land. This is also in full harmony with what is said in v. 3, where the carrying power of his voice bearing this world-wide message is

likened to the roaring of a lion (cf. for similar imagery
Hos. 11:10; Amos 3:8; 1 Pet. 5:8). Just what this angel
uttered in his loud cry is not definitely stated; but while
it is a message of divine judgment, it is also a message
of grace, open, clear, plain, and comprehensible to all men.
The effect of the angel's cry was that it was followed by
the utterance of their voices by the seven thunders (cf.
4:5; 8:5). These thunders, seven in number as denoting
the relation between God and the world, indicate the
majesty of God, relate the contents of this little book, and
confirm the cry of this mighty angel (cf. Ps. 29:5). Here
these thunder voices bearing the divine message come in
their full strength with the last decisive warning.

V. 4 shows that these thunders did not merely make
a reverberating noise, but gave forth an articulate message — an utterance which John was about to write down.
What they uttered, they spoke in unison; but just what
their words were, we are not told. This was not a revelation which John was then to record or make known.
A voice from heaven ordered him to seal those things the
seven thunders had spoken and not to write them down.
Why this prohibition was given, we do not know. It is
not necessary for us to know all the mysteries and secrets
of the future. It is sufficient for us as believers to
know that God's promises are ever dependable, absolutely
trustworthy; and that they will never fail us, however
great and severe may be our trials and conflicts with the
deceptive forces of the world.

In vv. 5-6 attention is again directed to this angel with
the open book in hand as the bearer of the divine message
confirming the inviolableness of all the prophetic promises
and their unconditional fulfillment independent of all
time. The posture of this angel indicates that his voice
encompasses both land and sea, thus embracing the whole

world, to which his words are addressed. In the description of him as lifting up his right hand to heaven, there is
described the usual manner of taking an oath. Since the
oath of this angel is altogether concerned about this little
book, it is quite appropriate that the angel should raise
the same hand in which this little book is held. The vital
importance of this little book is not to be lost sight of in
this vision. With uplifted hand swearing by the Ever-
living One, with whom all time is an eternal now, this
angel stands now, after the six angels have sounded their
trumpets and the last warnings to the earth dwellers have
gone forth unheeded, and directly announces the fulfillment of the divine decree which has been laid down in
the prophetic Word of all time. God is here described
also as the Creator of all things in the universe. This
corresponds exactly with the account of creation as given
in the first words of the first book of the Bible and won-
derfully confirms it. This is manifestly a strong condemnation of the denial of the creation by God of all that
exists. The brief but extremely important message which
this angel has to deliver is that time shall no longer exist.
Time, which began at creation, will cease when the consummation of the age has been reached. But up to the
final Judgment the curse of delusion which the sixth
trumpet announces will continue. In Dan. 12:7 we have
a somewhat similar apocalyptic vision; but the reference
there is to a definite period and not to the end of time.
This vision is certainly an awe-inspiring one.

In v. 7 reference is made to the beginning of the
sounding of the trumpet by the last of the seven trumpet
angels. In the opening words, "but in the days of the
voice of the seventh angel," there is no intimation that
the seventh angel sounds the trumpet continuously. The
expression "in the days" refers to the whole period covered by these seven visions of the trumpet-sounding

angels. In the words: "when he was about to sound the trumpet," attention is directed to the time when the angel is on the point of sounding the trumpet. This notable event marks the finishing, or completion, of the mystery of God and places us at the end of time. This is called a mystery because it is something that is unknown to the world and unknown also to believers save as it is revealed to them in the Holy Scriptures. The words: "as He hath declared to His servants, the prophets," are added to show that this revelation contained in the little book in the angel's right hand is in no respect different from the eternally time-honored prophetic Word. God's servants include all true believers; but the word "prophets" is added here to indicate that not all true believers are meant, but only those to whom God entrusted His revelation in the Old Testament and in the New Testament, to be conveyed by them to their fellow men. The object of this revelation is that bringing of the mystery of the Gospel to its final consummation; and its purpose is the delivering of human beings out of spiritual darkness into the glorious light of Christ's kingdom. Now the same angel which John heard in v. 4, prohibiting him from writing down what the seven thunders had uttered, he hears again, this time commanding him to take the little book held open in the hand of the mighty angel, pictured again as standing on the sea and on the earth, thus indicating the universality of its message for the whole world of mankind. To the angel's command John yielded implicit obedience, requesting him to give the little book to him. To this request the angel immediately replied with the injunction: "Take it and eat it up," i. e., digest it and become united with its contents (for a somewhat similar picture compare Ezek. 2:8-9; 3:1-3). At the same time the angel informs John of the effect the eating of the little book will have upon him. It will be bitter to him as he endures tribulations and afflictions in this life for the sake of the Gospel message, with which he is now identified. But on the other hand it will be sweet to him as he confesses with his mouth the glorious Gospel of Jesus Christ, the Gospel of life and everlasting salvation. In the tenth verse of this chapter, John relates his experience of the effects that followed upon his eating of the little book. He declares that he found it even as the angel had said, sweet in his mouth, but bitter in his stomach.

In the last verse, John, who has digested the little book and identified himself with its contents, is enjoined to prophesy and carry its gracious message far and wide, wherever the peoples of the earth may be found. This is in full accord with the Lord's own words: "And this Gospel of the Kingdom shall be preached in all the world for a witness unto all nations, and then shall the end come" (Matt. 24:14).

Chapter 11

1. *And there was given me a reed like unto a rod; and the angel stood, saying: Rise, and measure the temple of God, and the altar, and them that worship therein.* 2. *But the court which is without the temple leave out and measure it not, for it is given unto the Gentiles; and the Holy City shall they tread under foot forty and two months.* 3. *And I will give power unto My two witnesses, and they shall prophesy a thousand two hundred and threescore days, clothed in sackcloth.* 4. *These are the two olive trees and the two candlesticks standing before the God of the earth.* 5. *And if any man will hurt them, fire proceedeth out of their mouth and devoureth their enemies; and if any man will hurt them, he must in this manner be killed.* 6. *These have power to shut heaven, that it rain not in the days of their prophecy, and have power over waters to turn them to blood and to smite the earth with all plagues as*

often as they will. 7. And when they shall have finished their tes-
timony, the beast that ascendeth out of the bottomless pit shall
make war against them and shall overcome them and kill them.
8. And their dead bodies shall lie in the street of the great city,
which spiritually is called Sodom and Egypt, where also our Lord
was crucified. 9. And they of the people and kindreds and tongues
and nations shall see their dead bodies three days and an half and
shall not suffer their dead bodies to be put in graves. 10. And they
that dwell upon the earth shall rejoice over them and make merry
and shall send gifts one to another, because these two prophets
tormented them that dwelt on the earth. 11. And after three days
and an half the Spirit of Life from God entered into them, and they
stood upon their feet; and great fear fell upon them which saw
them. 12. And they heard a great voice from heaven saying unto
them: Come up hither. And they ascended up to heaven in a
cloud, and their enemies beheld them. 13. And the same hour was
there a great earthquake, and the tenth part of the city fell, and in
the earthquake were slain of men seven thousand; and the remnant
were affrighted and gave glory to the God of heaven. 14. The
second woe is past; and, behold, the third woe cometh quickly.
15. And the seventh angel sounded; and there were great voices in
heaven, saying: The kingdoms of this world are become the king-
doms of our Lord and of His Christ; and He shall reign forever and
ever. 16. And the four and twenty elders which sat before God
on their seats fell upon their faces and worshiped God, 17. saying:
We give Thee thanks, O Lord God Almighty, which art, and wast,
and art to come, because Thou hast taken to Thee Thy great power
and hast reigned. 18. And the nations were angry, and Thy wrath
is come, and the time of the dead that they should be judged, and
that Thou shouldest give reward unto Thy servants, the prophets,
and to the saints, and them that fear Thy name, small and great;
and shouldest destroy them which destroy the earth. 19. And the
temple of God was opened in heaven, and there was seen in His
temple the Ark of His testament; and there were lightnings and
voices and thunderings and an earthquake and great hail.

This chapter continues the vision given in the preceding chapter. In it John describes his own participation in symbolical acts pertaining to the Church. Taking the little book and eating it, he prophesies to many peoples, nations, tongues, and kings. In the first section of this chapter, down to v. 13 inclusive, we see him measuring the Church and marking the boundary line between it and the world.

In v. 1 he tells us how he was equipped for the work before him, saying: "And there was given me a reed like unto a rod." By whom this was done is not stated; but there can be no doubt that it was by the Lord. That a reed should be thus used is due to its resemblance to a rule or measuring rod. There follows immediately the command of the angel to John to be up and doing the task set before him. This task is to measure "the temple and the altar and the worshipers therein." These terms symbolize the one holy Christian Church consisting of true believers and separate from the world and from all that is outside of itself. The measuring rod is symbolical of the Gospel, the "little book," whose contents God ordered to be prophesied over the whole wide world (cf. 10:11). The result of this was the creation of the Church. Those who remained outside are the earth dwellers, upon whom the curses of the six trumpet judgments fall. These judgments of delusion are briefly but adequately described by St. Paul in 2 Thess. 2:11-12. What John is to measure here are not three distinct things, viz., temple, altar, and worshipers, but one thing only, viz., the Church.

In v. 2 John is directed to leave out and not to measure anything that is outside the Church, or not connected with it. The outer court of the Jewish Temple, as the court of the Gentiles, is symbolical of all that is unholy or belonging to the world. This he is to reject as profane and as in no way belonging to the Church. The reason assigned for this is that this court is given to the heathen, i. e., to all outside the Church. Such can in no sense be accepted as worshipers at the altar of the Lord. John expands this symbolism of the outer court by adding:

"and the Holy City they shall tread down forty-two months." The words "the Holy City" refer to Jerusalem, here characterized as holy, as the place where God had placed His name and as the site of His Temple, where the worship of the true God was carried on (cf. the words of the Lord Himself, Luke 21:24). As a matter of fact this Jerusalem, rejected of God, is trodden down by the Gentiles unto this day. The period of forty-two months is also to be understood symbolically. This number designates the time referred to by Christ in the words: "till the times of the Gentiles be fulfilled" — the end of the present dispensation, when the seventh trumpet sounds the last woe (see vv. 14-19). There is here no intimation of the conversion of the whole nation of the Jews. The various designations of "the times of the Gentiles," as three and one-half years, forty-two months, and one thousand, two hundred, and sixty days, are impressive. The picture of the heathen as ruling for three and one-half years is terrible. Still more terrible is the description of them as ruling forty-two months. And most terrible of all is the description of their reign as continuing one thousand, two hundred, and sixty days without intermission as day follows upon day.

From v. 3 to v. 14 is given a description of the Lord's witnesses. The Lord has His witnesses, as the parting words to His disciples clearly show: "And ye shall be witnesses unto Me both in Jerusalem and in all Judea and in Samaria and unto the uttermost part of the earth" (Acts 1:8). The question naturally arises: Who are they whom the Lord here designates in the expression "My two witnesses"? In answer we may say: This certainly does not refer to two actual men, whether Enoch and Elijah or Moses and Elijah, as some commentators conjecture. It is well known to readers of the Bible that, for the establishment of the truth on any matter brought forward for judgment, at least two witnesses are required (cf. Deut. 17:6; 19:15; Matt. 18:16; John 8:17). It is in this sense, therefore, that this expression is used here. These two witnesses typify the believing congregation, or the Church of true believers, which ever bears witness of Christ to the whole world. These two witnesses supplied by the Lord bear testimony that cannot be set aside without bringing condemnation upon all who reject their witness. And when it is said here that they shall prophesy, the meaning is that their witnessing is not mere human testimony, but that of divinely commissioned prophets. They testify to Christ's own Word, to the contents of the little book held open in the angel's right hand. The limitation of their prophesying to one thousand two hundred and sixty days corresponds to "the times of the Gentiles," i. e., of the heathen. This means that it runs through the entire present dispensation. The description of these two witnesses as clothed in sackcloth is significant, sackcloth being a symbol of repentance. The testimony of the Church to all outside of it is a call to repentance. Those outside the Church of true believers shall perish, not because no witness has been borne to them, but because they rejected the testimony and gave no heed to the call to repent. Just as Jerusalem killed the prophets sent to her and finally put Jesus Himself to death on the Cross, so has the world today, sunken as it is in heathenism, become Jerusalem in type. The picture here is a revelation of the guilt of the wicked world, which brings on the final Judgment. The very Gospel, which is a savor of life unto life to the believer, is a savor of death unto death to the unbeliever; and the Church, which is figured by the two witnesses, will continue this witness to the Word until its witness is supplanted according to God's eternal decree by the witness of suffering and death, when the witnessing Church shall go the way of its Lord and Master.

In v. 4 a symbolic explanation of the significance of these two witnesses is given similar to that employed by Zechariah (see Zech. 4:3, 11, 14), with this difference: that in the Zechariah passage there is only one candlestick instead of two; and that the two olive trees are represented as supplying the lamps with oil, whereas here the two trees and the two candlesticks are paralleled.

Besides this, in Zech. 4:14 it is stated that these olive trees are the anointed ones that stand before the Lord of the whole earth, while here the two olive trees and the two candlesticks are represented as standing by the Lord of the earth. Their standing by the Lord of the earth signifies that their witness is for the whole world (cf. v. 9; 10:11). This description makes it quite clear that no two individual persons are meant, but that it applies to the witnessing Church.

In the next verse we have a description of the miraculous power with which these two witnesses are endowed and by which they attest their divine commission and ward off their enemies until their testimony is finished. Their enemies are here characterized as those who are bent upon seeking their hurt. By the fire proceeding out of their mouth and devouring their enemies is symbolized the Word, which with its fire of judgment consumes its enemies (cf. Jer. 5:14). To make this still more emphatic, it is added: "and if any man will hurt them, he must in this manner be killed." The reference here is to the Word that proceedeth out of the mouth of the Lord's two witnesses, which in its fiery judgments destroys its enemies. This affords wonderful encouragement to the believing congregation, assuring it that in the midst of the greatest assault of the world spirit upon it the conquering strength of its testimony shall never fail. This promise in reference to the beacon light of Christian witness has great significance for believers of all time, and so also for us today.

when the enemies of Christ and His Church are so
rampant and bold.

In v. 6 the amazing power of these two witnesses is
vividly pictured as the stopping of rain by the locking up
of the heaven, by the turning of the waters into blood,
and by the smiting of the earth with every plague as often
as they wish. The symbolism here is taken from the action of Elijah, described in 1 Kings 17:1, and from that of
Moses in the ten plagues visited upon Egypt (Ex. 7:19).
There is, however, no ground for the inference drawn by
many commentators that these great personages will re-
appear and repeat their miracles upon this earth. Significance attaches only to such might and power as Elijah
and Moses manifested. These two great men had to deal
with the hardness of heart characterizing the people of
their day. The situation here is the same, having to deal
with those who, as belonging to the court outside the
Temple, are described as treading down the Holy City,
or in other words, as the enemies of God, whose guilt
brings in the last woe, the final Judgment. The prophesying of these witnesses is the prophesying of the true
Church, which by means of the Gospel bears constant
witness to the hardened and hostile world and brings its
guilt to light (cf. Matt. 24:14). The symbolism here
points to terrifying New Testament judgments not further
described beyond the fact that they are powers of judgment connected with the witnesses who proclaim God's
Word. These judgments are terrible in their nature. The
Word of the Lord will strike down His enemies. "It is a
fearful thing to fall into the hands of the living God"
(Heb. 10:31). When it is further said that these witnesses
have power to smite the earth with all manner of plagues
as often as they wish, it does not mean that they act
arbitrarily in administering their afflictions. As God's
servants (10:7) they do all that they do at His will. This

could not be otherwise, because the witness which they bear is His Word.

The words from v. 7 to v. 13 inclusive are words addressed to John by the angel indicated in v. 1. In the first of this group of verses it is shown that the Gospel testimony of these two witnesses revealing the guilt of the world will eventually be finished, and that whenever, and not before, this period arrives, their testimony will cease. This is in full accord with the Lord's own prediction in Matt. 24:14, where He tells us that the Gospel of the Kingdom is to be preached in the whole inhabited world as a testimony to all nations before the end shall come. No hostile power in the world shall be able to silence this testimony before the end of witness-bearing determined by the Lord is reached. The silencing of the testimony of these two witnesses will not be brought about by the unbelieving men whom this testimony condemns; but, as we are here explicitly told, by the beast that cometh up out of the abyss. This beast is characterized in these words as coming out of his home in hell. It is further declared that he shall do battle with these two witnesses and shall conquer and kill them. The important thing here is that their testimony, having reached the goal determined by the Lord, is finally silenced. The end will then be at hand, and the mystery of God as revealed in the Gospel will be finished. There is no use in speculating, as is done by many commentators, as to who this monster, called the beast, is. This beast, as Chapters 13 and 17 indicate, symbolizes the antichristian power as a whole dominating the world. This would include the Roman Antichrist personified in the Pope, the pagan and the atheistic world powers exercising their governmental authority under the direction of Satan, the Modernists with their denial of divine inspiration of the Scriptures, and the naturalists and materialists with their rejection

of the supernatural together with all others who undermine Christianity and tend to silence its gracious saving
message.

In the next verse we are told that the dead bodies of
these two witnesses are not allowed to be placed in a
tomb, but remain unburied in the broad street of Jerusalem, the typical world city where they had carried on
their testimony. This was the most monstrous outrage
that could be visited upon them. The city here called
"the great city" is the same as "the Holy City" mentioned
in v. 2. The city of Jerusalem as the site of our Lord's
crucifixion becomes the symbol of the city of the beast,
and as the seat of the attacks of the beast against the
Church and its testimony is here very appropriately
named "the great city." Of this great city it is stated
that it was called in a spiritual sense "Sodom and Egypt."
The undeniable fact that no city on earth was ever called
by such name makes it clear that no literal city is meant.
And the addition of the words: "where also our Lord was
crucified," is still further evidence of the figurative use
of these names. Sodom and Egypt, noted for their obduracy and for their enmity against the true and only
God, are fitting types of obduracy at its summit, such
as was exhibited in Jerusalem in the violent death upon
the Cross of the Lord Jesus Christ, whereby His bitter
enemies sought to stifle His prophetic voice. But let us
not forget that the same obduracy is prevalent today en-
deavoring to stifle the voice of the Gospel and smother
it in the blood of its witnesses. Only with the coming of
the final Judgment at the sounding of the seventh trumpet
will the Gospel testimony have reached its end.

Further description is given in v. 9, where the city is
conceived of as being made up of "people and tribes and
tongues and nations," forming one single hardened mass,
thus constituting it a veritable Sodom and Egypt. For

three and one-half days, symbolizing the half of God's
dealing with His slain witnesses, their dead bodies lie in
the broad street of the city in full view of all men, and
their corpses are not allowed to be placed in a tomb.
Thus do the enemies of God and His Word manifest
their extreme hatred of it and its testimony. They dis-
honor its witnesses and gloat over the fact that their
voices are now silenced and never again to be heard, as
they think. The rejoicing of the earth dwellers over the
death of the two witnesses is aptly described in the next
verse together with the reason occasioning it. The frequently recurring expression: "they that dwell on the
earth," designates those whose sole home is this earth
and who have no connection whatever with heaven.
Whether any believers will be left, when the last of the
seven trumpets sounds, who will mourn over the witnesses is questionable. Our Lord's own words in Luke
18:8 show at any rate that they will be exceedingly few.
The reason for the joyous celebration of these earth
dwellers is their deliverance from these tormenting
prophets. Jubilation reigns on earth when the Word of
the prophets is at last silenced.

V. 11 sets forth the remaining three and one-half days
of God's dealing with the two witnesses and discloses
what occurred to them in God's miraculous dealing with
them. It clearly shows that all the powers of evil combined are too feeble to conquer the Word. "Truth crushed
to earth shall rise again. The eternal years of God are
hers." Just as in the beginning God breathed into man's
body the breath of life, so here the Spirit of Life from
God enters into these two witnesses symbolizing His
everlasting Gospel to the consternation and terror of the
men of the world. The earth dwellers seeing these witnesses standing upon their feet could not deny that they
had been raised and were alive again. So terrific was the

effect upon them that they were overwhelmed with fear and dread.

In the succeeding verse further account is given of these two witnesses so miraculously made alive. They heard a great voice from heaven commanding them to ascend to heaven. This signifies that they have accomplished the task assigned to them, that their work is now finished, and that the Word is withdrawn forever from those who hated it and with murderous malignity sought to silence it. This voice, the same as in v. 1, these witnesses heard and immediately obeyed. The Lord who gave these witnesses (v. 3) finally withdraws them forever from those who will not heed their testimony. The door of God's grace is now shut to all eternity. This imagery teaches that the Word, through which alone salvation is brought to men, has finished its course in this world and will no more be offered to men, but that they will be left to reap the just consequences of their sin and guilt. The description of the immediate obedience of the two witnesses to their Lord's command is now given, reminding us of the account of the Lord's own ascension (Acts 1:9). These two prophets will be exalted to the glories in heaven, and the enemies will realize that the Word of God, the Gospel of everlasting salvation, is finally removed from them forever. The hour of salvation is past. It is now too late for those who persistently rejected the Word and put it from them to enter into the heavenly bridal chamber, however persistently they may henceforth knock. The Lord's answer to the obdurate enemies of His Word is the glorification of His Word in their sight and the filling of their hearts with terror and despair in view of the final Judgment pronounced by His Word. This is a reminder that "it is a fearful thing to fall into the hands of the living God."

V. 13 graphically describes the catastrophe that im-

mediately followed the ascension of the two witnesses, or
the withdrawal of the Word. A great earthquake strikes
this city which is the center and seat of opposition to
God — a reminder to us that there can be no greater
catastrophe than the removal of God's Word from the
world. The effects of this so great earthquake are described as the falling of the tenth of the city and the
killing of 7,000 human beings. As ten is the number of
completeness, this implies that final Judgment, or complete destruction, has not yet come, but only a minor
judgment, or partial destruction. The mentioning of 7,000
killed is not to be taken literally, but only indicates that
this judgment was not complete. In the words that follow
we have a description of the effect of this catastrophe
upon those that were not destroyed by it. Of them it is
asserted that they were terrified and gave glory to the
God of heaven. This must not be misinterpreted to mean
that they repented of their sins and became converted,
and that consequently the majority of this spiritual Sodom
and Egypt saw the error of their ways and became believers and were saved. This is impossible in view of the
fact that the Word has departed from them and the Holy
Ghost has withdrawn His gracious presence. Men can
never by their own powers believe in Jesus Christ or confess Him as their Lord. The very description of God, not
as their Lord or their God, but as "the God of heaven," is
an intimation of the non-conversion of this remnant. The
meaning here is that these enemies of God, who are under
the power of the spirit of the abyss, are terror-stricken as
the judgment of God descends upon them; and in their
alarming fright they acknowledge that this can come from
no other source than the God of heaven. God's judgments
apart from the Word will bring no one to repentance
(cf. 9:21).

V. 14 informs us that the second woe is now a thing

of the past, but that the third woe follows quickly upon it.
At v. 14 begins the account of the sounding of the trumpet
by the last of the seven trumpet angels. This brings to
a climax the trumpet judgments, just as was the case with
the seventh seal and, as we shall see later on, with the
seventh bowl. These three classes of seven judgments
cover the same ground, the seventh in each case taking
us to the end. It is simply impossible to conceive of them
as occurring in chronological order. Now we are told
what immediately followed the sounding of this last
trumpet, viz.: "and there occurred great voices in heaven."
It is foolish to speculate upon this and to say that John
was now removed from earth to heaven or that he trans-
ports himself into the future following the general Judgment. John is still "in spirit," as in 1:2 and 4:2. This is a
prophetic vision, and only what is revealed in the vision
is of importance. This being a vision of eternity when
time is no more (10:6), the time of the occurrence of the
things envisioned does not enter into consideration. The
description of these heavenly voices as "great voices"
signifies that they are not to be limited in any way, as,
e. g., to the voices of the Reformation heroes, but include
all the inhabitants of heaven, both saints and angels. All
join in the heavenly chorus proclaiming that the kingdom
of this world in which Satan usurped rule as its prince is
now a thing of the past, and that kingship over the world
henceforth belongs exclusively to "our Lord and His
Christ," i. e., to God and Christ. The implication here is
that all things have been made new and that God has
taken up His tabernacle among men, as is expressly declared in 21:1-5. The mystery of God is now finished; the
final consummation has arrived; and the Lord God omnipotent reigneth. The action of the twenty-four elders,
representatives of the Word of God in heaven, is now
described. As they see God's judgment carried out in all

its completion upon the enemies of His Word and His Church, they fall down upon their faces in deepest adoration and give thanks to Him who has taken retributive vengeance on all the suppressors of His Word and oppressors of His Church, and who has gloriously rewarded His saints.

In the next verse we have the record of their thanksgiving, expressing the gratitude of the entire Church to God for His action against its enemies. Their designation of God here is similar to that in 1:4 and 8 and other passages in Revelation, only that the words "and art to come" are omitted, and this for the reason that God's coming has now been accomplished in the retribution meted out to His enemies and in the eternal reward bestowed upon His believing people. The occasion for their thanksgiving is stated in the words: "because Thou hast taken to Thee Thy great power and hast reigned." This of course does not mean that God did not possess this power heretofore, even when He allowed the anti-Christian forces to do their worst against Him and His Church, but that now He has executed the power of His wrath in the final Judgment in destroying those who destroyed the earth. The statement here is, that God has put His omnipotent power to exercise without restraint. Now no longer to all eternity will Satan and his satellites be allowed to disturb the serenity of the blessedness of God's saints who have entered upon the enjoyment of their heavenly inheritance. The effect of all this upon God's enemies is next described. The anger of the heathen bursts rabidly forth against God and His Anointed One because of His righteous judgments and dealings in pouring out His wrath in all its fullness upon His enemies; but their anger is futile and cannot change in the least degree the horrible situation that confronts them. The final Judgment is further described as "the time of the dead that they should be judged," reminding us of John 5:28, and as the time of the dispensing of His eternal rewards. At the same judgment in which God sentences the wicked to eternal punishment He bestows the glorious rewards of His grace upon the blessed. Among these latter are mentioned first the prophets, who not only accepted God's will for themselves, but also zealously proclaimed it to others. In the words "to those that fear Thy name" are included all true believers, as the words "both small and great" strongly emphasize. In the last words of this verse the final destruction of the ungodly is set forth. They are here represented as receiving exact justice and as reaping the due reward of their sins. Those who destroyed the earth are now themselves destroyed by God, their Judge, all of whose judgments are holy and righteous.

The last verse of this chapter discloses a vision of the temple of God in heaven and of the ark forming its center. This does not mean that there is an actual temple or an actual ark in heaven. We must remember that this is a vision. What is important here is that the temple was opened, and that for the purpose of exposing the ark, its center. This ark was not veiled, covered, or concealed, but was seen. The ark of the covenant which God made with Abraham and the Children of Israel was symbolical of God's gracious promise made to them to send His Son as the Messiah for the expiation of the sin of the world and to rule forever as their Savior-King. What John sees here is the fulfillment and final consummation of this gracious promise with all that it involves. God's everlasting kingdom is now here. The mystery, God's whole plan of salvation, has been finished. The kingdom of the world has become the Kingdom of God and His Christ, and the last Judgment has been held. The accompanying phenomena described as "lightnings and voices and thunderings and an earthquake and great hail" are not natural things, but symbols denoting God's omnipotent power in action accomplishing the consummation of His grace for all His saints and the manifestation of His destroying power against the ungodly. These forceful phenomena leaving so much destruction in their wake are symbolical of God's omnipotent power. This completes the seventh trumpet vision; yet all that follows in this wonderful book is closely connected with it as showing still further revelations of the same thing with which this seventh trumpet vision deals.

Chapter 12

1. *And there appeared a great wonder in heaven; a woman clothed with the sun, and the moon under her feet, and upon her head a crown of twelve stars;* 2. *and she, being with child, cried, travailing in birth, and pained to be delivered.* 3. *And there appeared another wonder in heaven; and, behold, a great red dragon, having seven heads and ten horns, and seven crowns upon his heads.* 4. *And his tail drew the third part of the stars of heaven and did cast them to the earth; and the dragon stood before the woman which was ready to be delivered for to devour her child as soon as it was born.* 5. *And she brought forth a man-child, who was to rule all nations with a rod of iron; and her child was caught up unto God and to His throne.* 6. *And the woman fled into the wilderness, where she hath a place prepared of God, that they should feed her there a thousand two hundred and three-score days.* 7. *And there was war in heaven: Michael and his angels fought against the dragon; and the dragon fought and his angels,* 8. *and prevailed not, neither was their place found any more in heaven.* 9. *And the great dragon was cast out, that old serpent, called the devil and Satan, which deceiveth the whole world; he was cast out into the earth, and his angels were cast out with him.* 10. *And I heard a loud voice saying in heaven: Now is come salvation and strength and the Kingdom of our God and the power of His Christ;*

for the accuser of our brethren is cast down, which accused them before our God day and night. 11. And they overcame him by the blood of the Lamb and by the word of their testimony; and they loved not their lives unto the death. 12. Therefore rejoice, ye heavens, and ye that dwell in them. Woe to the inhabiters of the earth and of the sea! For the devil is come down unto you, having great wrath, because he knoweth that he hath but a short time. 13. And when the dragon saw that he was cast unto the earth, he persecuted the woman which brought forth the man-child. 14. And to the woman were given two wings of a great eagle that she might fly into the wilderness, into her place, where she is nourished for a time and times and half a time, from the face of the serpent. 15. And the serpent cast out of his mouth water as a flood after the woman that he might cause her to be carried away of the flood. 16. And the earth helped the woman, and the earth opened her mouth and swallowed up the flood which the dragon cast out of his mouth. 17. And the dragon was wroth with the woman and went to make war with the remnant of her seed, which keep the Commandments of God and have the testimony of Jesus Christ.

This chapter stands in close connection with both what precedes and what follows. The visions following the seventh trumpet vision now completely cover the same ground, but throw new and fuller light upon it. The first vision here, that of the woman and the dragon, pictorially describes all the efforts of Satan directed against Jesus Christ and His Church throughout the entire New Testament dispensation. What is offered in this vision is designated in v. 1 as a "sign"; and that not indeed a common or ordinary sign, but a "great sign" with its location in heaven. This expression indicates symbolism of the highest importance and significance. The woman here appearing is depicted as gorgeously arrayed, having the sun for her clothing with its beaming rays of light streaming forth all around her, with the moon for her footstool, and with a crown of twelve stars upon her head, thus presenting a majestic picture of heavenly splendor. The twelve stars symbolize the Church, not, however, the Church on earth, where her splendor is concealed, but the Church in heaven, where her glory shines forth in all its fullness. The picturing of the Church under the image of a woman is not unusual in the Scriptures (cf. Matt. 13:33; Luke 15:8; Ps. 45:13).

The second verse pictures this woman as pregnant and as suffering the perils and pains of childbirth — a torment that is now on the point of ending in the most blessed giving of birth. The reference in this is to the incarnation of the Son of God and is a fulfillment of the Prot-Evangelium (First Gospel), Gen. 3:15, the promise concerning "the Seed of the woman."

In the next verse there appears another sign also occurring in heaven — so described because the dragon appears here in heavenly light as he really is, stripped of all the deceiving splendor by which he formerly transformed himself into an angel of light. This dragon is further described as a great dragon, fiery red in color, and as having seven heads and ten horns, and seven crowns or diadems on his heads. Certainly such a monster cannot be conceived of as actually existing. The features just enumerated are purely symbolical. This dragon is evidently the devil (cf. v. 9; also the account of the temptation in Genesis 3). The number seven in connection with the heads and the diadems is a holy number, three for God and four for the world, and represents God in His dealings with the world of men. The devil thus described is pictured as usurping the divine majesty and power that belong to God in His relation to the world. The heads, symbols of royalty, in connection with the diadems upon them represent royal majesty and rule. The number ten, the number of completeness, together with the horns, symbolizes power — the complete power arrogated by Satan in his usurped dominion over men. This whole scene pictures Satan as presenting himself as God and demanding worship of men just as he did of Christ in the temptation (cf. Matt. 4:9).

In the next verse we have a further description of this dragon. Like the locusts in 9:10, he is represented as having power in his tail. The tearing away and casting down to earth of a third of the stars of heaven by the swishing of his tail is a dramatic description of this dragon's destructive power. In the last words of this verse the purpose of this mighty dragon is vividly set forth. Standing before the woman travailing in her birth-giving agonies, his purpose was to accomplish at all hazards the destruction of the Child that is on the point of being born. The stars of heaven in the preceding expression of this verse represent the holy angels whom Satan drew astray from God and cast down. The woman in the succeeding part of this verse is the Church, pregnant with the promise of the Messiah given from Gen. 3:15 on through the Old Testament Scriptures. The Child which she is about to bear is none other than Christ Himself, whose incarnation is here prefigured. Satan's whole policy is bent on the destruction of this Child, this Messiah.

In v. 5 we have set forth the birth of Christ, not historically of course, but in vision, including in its scope the whole presence of Christ on earth as the Messiah. Satan's presence before the woman and his purpose to destroy this Child is amply attested in the Gospel records (see Matt. 2:16-20; Luke 13:31; Acts 4:25-27). What is said here is in full accord with Old Testament prophecies of Christ's birth (cf. Is. 66:7; Ps. 2:7). The millenarian interpreters refer the ruling of Christ here with a rod of iron to the events pertaining to the time of the advent; but this is contrary to the meaning of Psalm 2. The only appropriate reference is to the entire New Testament era, during which Christ rules over the raging heathen with

the iron rod and defeats the counsels of their kings from
the time of His exaltation to the end. In the words that
follow, Christ's glorification is presented. This begins with
His ascension and includes His session at God's right
hand, from which He wields the iron rod of omnipotent
power till He subdues all enemies under His feet. In the
statement that this Child was snatched away unto God
and unto His throne, the agent implied is God (cf. Phil.
2:9; Heb. 1:4-14; 2:8-9). It is folly to apply this to the
elevation of Christianity to the throne of the Roman Empire in the time of Constantine, or with the millenarians
to postpone this rule of Christ to the time of His second
advent. What became of the woman when her Child was
rescued from the great red dragon is stated in v. 6. The
woman, who represents the Church, was not taken with
her Child into heaven; yet she, too, was in danger from
the dragon standing before her. The Church is to remain
on earth to fulfill the mission assigned to her by her Lord.
She escaped from the devouring dragon by fleeing into
the wilderness. This she did not on her own initiative, but
in full accord with God's own will and purpose; for there
God had prepared a place of refuge for her. God's purpose in this was not that she should rule over the nations
of the world in splendor and grandeur as do earthly kings,
or as the Pope aspires to do; but that in a place which
God Himself had prepared for her in the wilderness she
is to minister to God's little flock, which is ever under the
cross. There she is to be nourished for one thousand two
hundred and sixty days, or until her final redemption and
glorification at the end of the present dispensation. The
food by which she is nourished is the Word of God.

In vv. 7-9 is given a description of the effect and result
of the Savior's incarnation and subsequent enthronement,
illuminated in vv. 10-12 by the voice in heaven and its
song of triumph.

When in v. 7 it is said that there occurred war, or a battle, in heaven, this must not be interpreted to mean that a battle actually took place there, disturbing its peaceful serenity and its eternal, never-ending bliss — a thing which would be absolutely impossible. In this vision is described a supermundane battle somewhat similar to Paul's reference to the demons in heavenly places (Eph. 6:12). In this battle two forces are engaged, led on the one hand by Michael, the archangel (Jude 6), as general of the holy angels, and on the other by Satan as general of his evil angels. The holy angels are ever active in God's gracious dealing with men especially in times of crisis, as, e. g., at the birth, the resurrection, and the ascension of the Lord; and they will also accompany Him in His second coming in glory for judgment. Similarly the hellish hosts of wickedness under the command of the devil and with him battle viciously against Christ and His followers.

In the following verse is pictured the complete victory of Christ through His angel army over the devil and his hosts of darkness. In the added words: "neither was their place found any more in heaven," the meaning is not that before this or up to this time they had actually been in heaven, as they had lost this estate long ago, even before the fall of man; but the meaning is that the devil and his evil hosts, being utterly defeated, can no longer bring accusation before God against the believing Christian brethren (cf. Rom. 8:1, 33-34). The result of this battle and its significance for the devil and his angels is most forcefully brought out in v. 9, presenting a complete fulfillment of the Lord's own prophecy in John 12:31. The overwhelming and utter defeat of Satan and his angels is emphatically brought out by the threefold repetition of the verb "cast out," literally, "cast down"; and by the grouping together, as nowhere else in Scripture, of significant names descriptive of this great enemy of God and man. The name "dragon" has already been explained in v. 3. The name "old serpent" points back to the Genesis account (Genesis 3), where he is described as "more subtile than any beast of the field which the Lord had made." The name "devil" signifies "the slanderous one." And the name "Satan" means the "adversary," the one who lies in ambush for another. All these names apply to this chief of evil spirits with their fullest significance. To these names is added a description of the activity in which Satan is constantly engaged and to which he devotes all his energy and power. The casting of him and his angels down to the earth is incontrovertible proof of his overwhelming and utter defeat. The words "to the earth" are added, not to imply that he had a place in heaven or that he had succeeded in invading that holy realm, but only to show how far away he had been thrown.

V. 10, which now follows, introduces the song of triumph. John declares here that he heard "a great voice," which, like the great voices mentioned in 11:15, is in heaven. The message to which this great voice gives utterance explains and interprets the battle just described, which ended in the utter defeat and complete overthrow of Satan and his hosts of darkness. The utterance of this voice deals first with God and His Christ, then with believers, and finally with those in heaven and those on earth. The salvation which God has provided is the full salvation of believers. This has now reached its completion because their enemy, who accused them day and night before God, has been cast out. God's almighty power also has been manifested by the sending of His Son, the Son's incarnation, and in His subsequent exaltation and session at God's right hand, resulting in the utter defeat and overthrow of the dragon. The same is said likewise of the Kingdom of our God and the authority of

His Christ. The Kingdom of God is God's Kingdom of
Grace, in which He rules over the hearts and souls of believers, bestowing upon them His grace and salvation in
spite of all efforts of Satan to prevent it. The authority
of Christ is that which was given to Him according to
His human nature and of which He speaks in Matt. 28:18,
where He declares that all authority has been given unto
Him in heaven and in earth, which authority He exercises
also in His human nature. All this has now come to pass.
The voice of the accuser has been silenced forever. The
effect of these mighty deeds of God through the Son is to
make the salvation of believers sure and complete (cf.
Rom. 8:1; Luke 10:17-24).

In v. 11 the believers' conquest of Satan, the dragon, is
set forth. The believing people of God are pictured here
as standing before God's judgment seat to receive their
sentence. Their adversary and accuser having been cast
out, they have gained the victory over him. Assurance of
this is given in other New Testament passages, notably in
Rom. 8:33, 34, 37; 16:20. The cause occasioning the win-
ning of this victory is also clearly stated. It was not that
they had committed no sins, but that their sins were
atoned for in the blood of the Lamb (cf. 7:14). This is
the expiatory cause of their victory. A second reason is
added, viz., the Word of God and the testimony of Jesus
(cf. 1:9). The Word which they held by faith is the
mediatory cause of their victory over Satan, their in-
veterate foe. It is further pointed out that to these saints
their testimony was more precious than life itself. They
were ready to endure death in martyrdom rather than
to deny the Lord that bought them and the Word of their
testimony. Of this St. Paul furnishes a good example in
Acts 20:24, where he says: "Neither count I my life dear
to myself so that I might finish my course with joy," etc.

In the following verse we have the call by the voice

from heaven to celebrate the effect of Christ's enthronement. Both the heavens and those that dwell in them
are called upon to rejoice. By "those that dwell in the
heavens" human beings are meant, though angels also
take part in the celebration. Joy over the saved is so great
that the very heavens resound with the jubilation of its
inhabitants. But here another picture follows, the very
opposite of the preceding one. The same voice cries out
to all the earth dwellers proclaiming woe, which is the
portion of all the ungodly.

In v. 9 the devil is described as "cast down to the
earth"; but here it is said that he "went down." There is
no contradiction here, as the present account deals with
his voluntary activity in urging the earth dwellers into
great wrath against the Church of true believers on earth.
Why he is so zealous in this, is indicated in the last words
of this verse. He realizes that his season is short. He
must therefore diligently employ it for the accomplishment of his evil ends.

In v. 13 the history of the woman there described as
taking refuge in the wilderness is resumed. The devil,
realizing his utter defeat and his inability henceforth to
accuse the believers before God, now directs his malig-
nant persecution against the woman who gave birth to
the male Child snatched up into heaven, and so beyond
the reach of the dragon. This means that he pursued the
Church with full intent to destroy it. And this has indeed
been the devil's work ever since he failed in his effort to
destroy the Christ.

V. 14 furnishes an account of the woman's escape by
flight. The eagle imagery here has no connection with
that in 8:13, but is taken from Exod. 19:4 (cf. Is. 63:9).
To this woman were given, manifestly by God, two wings
of a great eagle for the purpose of securing her safety in

flight. The words "where she is nourished" look back
to v. 6, where both her flight into the wilderness and
God's purpose to nourish her there are stated explicitly.
The same period of nourishment is given in both verses,
although expressed in different terms (cf. 11:3). The
period indicated in each case is the entire period during
which the Church is under the cross, i. e., the present
dispensation. During this period the persecution or
tribulation of the Church, however great it may be, can
do her no harm, seeing that she is under God's almighty
protection in the place which God has provided for her
and where He nourishes her "away from the face of the
serpent," or in other words, where the serpent can neither
reach, touch, nor harm her. The number seven, as we
have frequently seen, represents God's providential protection of the Church. The half of this number indicated
in this verse implies God's providential dealing with His
New Testament Church.

Vv. 15 16 set forth the devil's mighty efforts to destroy
the Church and the gracious deliverance of the Church
from them. The imagery here is similar to that in Ps.
74:15. The repeated reference here to the mouth brings
the mouth of the dragon into the foreground. The devil
seeks to overwhelm and drown the Church by that which
he spews forth out of his mouth. The reference in this is
to his diabolical delusions of all kinds, whether in the
realm of religion, or of philosophy, or of science. All such
delusions are the outspewing of Satan, who leaves no
stone unturned to deceive the whole world and turn it
away from God. He even seeks to carry away the Church
of true believers by the enormous flood of delusions which
he pours forth after it. The rescue of the woman is next
described in the statement that the earth opened her
mouth and swallowed up the flood which the dragon cast
out of his mouth. This means that to the earth and its

earth dwellers the river of delusions spewed out of his
mouth by the devil was so welcome that it was at once
absorbed, while the Church on her powerful eagle wings
flies away so swiftly that these waters do not reach her.
This outpouring of delusions is continuous, and is not
limited to any particular time or event in the history of
the Church. Glimpses of it are in evidence in our day in
the spreading of such false views as Evolution, Christian
Science, Russellism, Mormonism, Secretism, Dowieism,
Rosicrucianism, and other monstrosities, which the ungodly world so readily accepts, but which altogether fail
to engulf the Church of true believers, which is ever under God's gracious protection.

In the last verse the impression which this made upon
the dragon is described. He is enraged over his failure to
accomplish the destruction of the woman. Previously he
had failed to destroy her Child. Now, that the woman
also escapes him exasperates him beyond measure. The
dragon, though thwarted in his attacks against the Church
as a whole, does not desist from his pernicious activity.
Bound to do all the evil he can, he leaves the pursuit of
the Church as a whole and directs his efforts toward accomplishing the destruction of the remaining ones of her
seed, namely, individual believers. These, begotten by
the Church through the means of grace, become the objects of his vicious attacks. But that he does not accomplish their destruction becomes clear from the description
of them as "those keeping the Commandments of God
and having the testimony of Jesus," i. e., the Gospel. Believing Christians having this testimony and keeping it in
their heart are objects of the attacks of Satan, but do not
succumb to his assaults. Out of these conflicts they come
forth more than conquerors through Jesus Christ, their
Lord.

Chapter 13

1. *And I stood upon the sand of the sea and saw a beast rise up out of the sea having seven heads and ten horns, and upon his horns ten crowns, and upon his heads the name of blasphemy. 2. And the beast which I saw was like unto a leopard, and his feet were as the feet of a bear, and his mouth as the mouth of a lion; and the dragon gave him his power and his seat and great authority. 3. And I saw one of his heads as it were wounded to death; and his deadly wound was healed; and all the world wondered after the beast. 4. And they worshiped the dragon which gave power unto the beast; and they worshiped the beast, saying: Who is like unto the beast? Who is able to make war with him? 5. And there was given unto him a mouth speaking great things and blasphemies, and power was given unto him to continue forty and two months. 6. And he opened his mouth in blasphemy against God, to blaspheme His name and His tabernacle and them that dwell in heaven. 7. And it was given him to make war with the saints and to overcome them, and power was given him over all kindreds and tongues and nations. 8. And all that dwell upon the earth shall worship him, whose names are not written in the Book of Life of the Lamb slain from the foundation of the world. 9. If any man have an ear, let him hear. 10. He that leadeth into captivity shall go into captivity; he that killeth with the sword must be killed with the sword. Here is the patience and the faith of the saints. 11. And I beheld another beast coming up out of the earth; and he had two horns like a lamb, and he spake as a dragon. 12. And he exerciseth all the power of the first beast before him and causeth the earth and them which dwell therein to worship the first beast, whose deadly wound was healed. 13. And he doeth great wonders so that he maketh fire come down from heaven on the earth in the sight of men, 14. and deceiveth them that dwell on the earth by the means of those miracles which he had power to do in the sight of the beast, saying to them that dwell on the earth that they should make an image to the beast which had the wound by a sword and did live. 15. And he had power to give life unto the image of the beast, that the image of the beast should both speak and cause that as many as would not worship the image of the beast should be killed. 16. And he*

*causeth all, both small and great, rich and poor, free and bond, to
receive a mark in their right hand or in their foreheads, 17. and
that no man might buy or sell save he that had the mark or the
name of the beast or the number of his name. 18. Here is wisdom.
Let him that hath understanding count the number of the beast;
for it is the number of a man; and his number is six hundred three-
score and six.*

This chapter presents a continuation of what is
contained in the preceding chapter. The chief
distinction here is that, whereas Chapter 12 gives account
of Satan's efforts to destroy Jesus Himself and then His
Church, in the present chapter he acts against the Church
through his agents, thus symbolizing the whole antichristian power directed against the saints of the Lord.
The same ground is covered as in 12:13-17, but is dealt
with more fully here and in greater detail. The activity of
these two beasts is not to be relegated to the future or
to what will take place shortly before the end or near
Christ's second coming. Neither is it to be limited to the
Moslem invasions or, as regards place, to the continent of
Europe. It indeed includes the whole period from Christ's
exaltation to the end of the world.

In v. 1 the best attested reading is "he stood" instead
of "I stood" (A. V.). The reference is to the dragon mentioned in 12:17. The dragon is described here as standing
on the sand of the sea because the sand is the place where
sea and land meet, and because, while the beast comes
up out of the sea, another of the dragon's beasts, mentioned later on, comes up out of the earth. The sea and
the earth mentioned here comprise the whole world. The
coming up of these beasts out of the sea and out of the
earth designates their source as being from beneath and
not from above. It is also implied that they do not arise
of themselves, but are the agents of Satan, who stands on

the shore of the sea. The name "beast" applies to each of them, designates them as cruel, destructive, ravenous, and frightful monsters, such as were never actually seen upon earth. The description of this first beast that follows is quite similar to the description of Satan in 12:3, except that there it is his heads and not his horns that bear the crowns or diadems. The numbers ten and seven are here, as elsewhere, symbolical, ten signifying the completeness of God's royal power in action and seven God's dealings with men, the implication being that these beasts' plans and designs bear resemblance to, but in reality are a counterfeit of, God's holy and sacred Word. The statement that these seven heads have on them names of blasphemy indicates that the horns bear names insulting to God as arrogating to the beast what actually belongs to God. Just what these names are is not stated.

In v. 2 is given a still further description of this horrible monster, combining in one three of the four frightful beasts described in the seventh chapter of Daniel. The combination thus applied is full of horror and indicates the source of all the power, rule, and authority exercised by this beast as not his own, but that of Satan, whose agent he is and in whose service he stands.

In the following verse John sees one of the seven heads of this beast slain unto death, whereby the beast himself was slain. Nothing is said as to who delivered this stroke or as to the time of its occurrence; but, properly understood, it fits well into the picture. This beast stands for the whole antichristian power which Satan as the prince of this world exerts. This antichristian power received its death stroke from Christ upon His exaltation and session at God's right hand, where He exercises all divine authority and dominion. The statement that his death stroke was healed implies that this beast became alive again. This was so, because the final Judgment had

not as yet occurred. On Christ's exaltation all enemies
had not yet been put under His feet. Satan, though cast
down (12:9), was still allowed to exercise his antichristian power in the world. But notwithstanding his unceasing activity, God has gathered and preserved His
saints in His holy Church. In the words "the whole
world wondered at the beast" we have a description of the
effect made by him upon the earth dwellers. In wonder
and amazement they gaze admiringly upon the power
present before their very eyes.

In the following verse explanation is given as to why
they worshiped the beast. It was because the dragon,
i. e., the devil, gave to him the authority which he manifests. In yielding to the antichristian power, men yield
to the dragon himself, whose agent the beast is. Having
given themselves to the worship of the dragon, it naturally follows that they worship his agent who derives all
his authority from him. In their worship they give expression to their estimation of the incomparable greatness
of the beast in the rhetorical questions: "Who is like unto
the beast? And who is able to make war with him?"

In v. 5 we have still more detailed description of this
beast. He is a creature and as such under God's control
and, therefore, can do only what God permits. It was
God who gave unto him a mouth and permitted him to
use it in uttering great things and blasphemies. Why God
did so is a mystery to us, just as is the case with the origin
of sin. While we may not comprehend it, God understands
it; and this should be sufficient for us. This beast is described here as uttering great things and blasphemies,
such as slandering God and reviling Him and all that He
holds sacred. This means that the whole antichristian
power is continuously and in countless ways pouring out
its blasphemous tirades against God and His Word. These
tirades cannot be limited to special times, special govern-

ments, or special persons, but go on without intermission. But the authority of this beast is not absolute. God, who permits it, also controls it and has set bounds to it. The beast is permitted to operate for forty-two months, the period of the present New Testament dispensation. Thereafter neither the dragon nor his agents can operate any more, although within this period their blasphemies cover the whole world.

In v. 6 is described the use which the beast makes of the mouth which has been given him. First of all his blasphemous utterances are directed against God. And who can measure the blasphemies of the whole anti-christian world against God with their denial of His existence, their denial of the Trinity, their denial of the revelation in Scripture, their denial of the Virgin Birth, their denial of the Blood Atonement, etc., etc., *ad infinitum!*

John now proceeds to emphasize and explain still further the nature of the blasphemies that come forth from the mouth of this beast that is so active in the world. The word "name" used in this connection means the Word of God. To speak against this Word is to blaspheme God, its Author, whose Holy Spirit always accompanies and animates it. The words "His tabernacle and those that dwell in heaven" refer to the saints in the Church Triumphant, to those who in this world have fought the good fight of faith and waged the good warfare and who, as 12:11 tells us, conquered on account of the blood of the Lamb and on account of their testimony. To speak against them and to dissuade men from following in their footsteps is to blaspheme God in a most pernicious manner; and yet how manifold and how great are such blasphemies in the world today!

In v. 7 is described what was given to this beast to do, viz., to engage in battle with the saints and to conquer them. In the eleventh verse of the preceding chapter, the saints are represented as conquering the beast, which they do in their blessed death. Here, however, the saints who are still on earth are portrayed as conquered through the harm, injury, and suppression which the arrogant, blasphemous beast inflicts, whereby their lives here on earth are tortured. It is shown further in this verse that the authority of this agent of the dragon extends over the whole world and over all nations, tribes, and classes of men. Throughout the whole wide world, which this beast dominates, much trouble is made for the saints, who constitute so small a flock in it.

V. 8 brings out the fact that this worship of the beast will not cease, but will continue as long as this world lasts, and that it will be indulged in by each and every one of the earth dwellers whose name has not been written in the Book of Life of the Lamb slain from the foundation of the world. The Book of Life here mentioned is the infallible record of the Lord's omniscience; it contains the names of all those who have true spiritual life. The ascription of this Book of Life to the Lamb slain from the foundation of the world is of profound significance. Christ was slain in God's eternal purpose from the foundation of the world, and the efficacy of His death extends backward as well as forward. Eternity is timeless, time itself being a creation of God. (Cf. 1 Pet. 1: 19-20; John 17:24; Eph. 1:4.)

The admonition that follows in v. 9 corresponds to the admonition at the close of each of the Lord's letters to the seven churches. Accordingly they are not the words of John, but an essential part of the vision calling for earnest consideration of all that is contained in it.

In v. 10 a vivid picture is given of the endurance and the faith of the saints. The translation of this verse in our English version is not accurate. In the original the sentence is conditional and should read: "If any one (goeth) into captivity, into captivity he goeth: if any one shall kill with the sword, it is necessary that he with the sword shall be killed." This is a sententious statement. It means that if any one lives like the earth dwellers just described, he goes into the captivity of hell, or eternal torment; and that if any one shall kill God's saints with an earthly sword, he shall be killed with the sword of God's justice, the sword that kills with eternal death. In this situation is manifested the patient endurance and the faith of the saints.

In vv. 11-18 we are given a description of the second beast. This beast was not different in character or nature from the beast just described. Serving the dragon in the same capacity as the former, he is simply called "another beast." The first one was seen by John as coming up out of the sea; this one he sees coming up out of the earth. There is no symbolism in the terms earth and sea; rather they are to be taken as embracing the whole world. In the description this second beast appears less harmful than the first beast with his seven heads and ten horns, bear's feet and lion's mouth. But, though he has only two horns like a lamb, the description of him as speaking like a dragon, i. e., like Satan, whose agent he is, shows that he is far from being as harmless as he appears.

In the next verse he is depicted as exercising all the authority of the first beast. This authority given by the dragon to the first beast passes from him to the second beast. All this authority the second beast uses under the eyes of the first beast, whose agent he is. The use to which he puts the authority given him is now stated. It is directed toward the earth and its inhabitants, the earth dwellers, who live for this world only. But all such are included. What he induces them to do is to worship the first beast, whose deadly wound was healed. The activity of this beast, who is a zealous worker in the cause of his master, is set forth in v. 13. There he is described as doing "great signs," signs extremely startling and calling forth admiration and wonder from all beholders. This reminds us of an actual miracle, recorded in 1 Kings 18:38, in confirmation of the worship of Jehovah as the only true God. But here the authority is not from God, but from the dragon; and the signs, though great, are not real miracles, but counterfeit miracles such as proceed from the spirit of deception and the father of lies. The climax of his great signs is his making fire come down from heaven before the very eyes of men. This does not imply an overwhelming conflagration. These signs, being the devil's signs, are comparatively insignificant.

In v. 14, which follows, the work of this beast is characterized as a work of deception. His great signs, being spurious, need to be supported by deceits of all kinds; whereas genuine miracles require no such support. Those whom he deceives are the earth dwellers. And all his signs, however great they may be, are under God's control. God's sovereignty is supreme; and the devil and his agents are powerless against it. In the last words of this verse the beast issues orders to his dupes, the earth dwellers, to construct an image of the beast who had suffered the stroke of the sword and lived. In ordering this image to be made the second beast is but performing his work of glorifying the first beast; and this reaches its climax in making this image an object of universal adoration. The reference in this verse is to the whole antichristian world power, struck down by Christ, as with the stroke of a sword, by His victory in accomplishing human redemption.

In the following verse we are told of still further power possessed by this beast. It was given to him to give breath to this image, and that for a twofold purpose: first, that this image might be enabled to speak — a thing which no other image was ever able to do; second, that those who would not worship the image of the beast should be killed. This would be a powerful incentive to the earth dwellers to render worship to it. (Cf. Daniel 3 for a similar situation.)

In vv. 16-17 we find still further emphasis on the activity of the beast, who is never idle in the service of the dragon. His influence is exerted on all the earth dwellers without exception. These are now enumerated in pairs, in which all classes and conditions of men are included. The first pair, being the most prominent, are named on an ascending scale; the next two on a descending scale. But this is without special significance, the only significant thing being that the enumeration is all-inclusive. The beast causeth all the earth dwellers to be branded with a mark on the most prominent part of their bodies, definitely indicating them as belonging to him and to the dragon, in whose service he is. This mark is the counterpart of God's sealing of His servants, the 144,000 saints of Chapter 7. The difference here is that God seals His servants, while the devil only marks his dupes; and that the sealing occurs in Christ's name, while the marking takes place in the name of the first beast, or the antichristian world power. A further burden is laid upon those who refuse to receive this mark. And as a matter of history, Christians through the ages have had to submit to the boycott of hatred and opposition on the part of the antichristian world power. The buying and selling here mentioned are symbols of such antagonisms. Those who submit to the mark are exempt from oppression by the beast and the dragon and their dupes. The name of the beast is defined as "the number of the name," the number constituting a mark of identification.

The last verse of this chapter directs attention to the seriousness of the situation confronting us, reminding us of Christ's words at the close of each of the seven letters: "He that hath an ear, let him hear." It is a command to every one who has a mind, or intelligence, to put it to use. What is here commanded us to do is to count the number of the beast. The reason for obeying this command, the ease with which this may be done, is added as an inducement to yield obedience to this requirement. That the expressions "the number of a man" is a mistranslation is evident from the fact that John has just mentioned it in this same sentence as "the number of the beast." Manifestly he could not contradict himself now and say that it is the number of a man. The correct translation here is "a human number." This number is also symbolical. Six is the number of incompleteness; and this number plus its multiple by ten, plus its multiple by ten times ten, expresses intensified incompleteness, as falling short three times of the number seven, which is the number of God, including Christ and all His grace and salvation for men. 666, on the other hand, is the number of the antichristian world power, stamping the earth dwellers as entirely outside the Kingdom of God and His Christ, and as doomed to final and complete defeat. The number 666 is not cabalistic or cryptic. It does not refer to any one individual, but to the world-wide opposition to God and His cause, characterizing all who bear this mark as belonging to the dragon and his kingdom of darkness.

In this chapter the first beast represents the whole antichristian power throughout the world. The second beast, who is in the service of the first beast, represents the whole antichristian propaganda that is carried on in the world. The first beast personifies ferocious power. The second beast personifies deceptive propaganda.

Chapter 14

1. And I looked, and, lo, a Lamb stood on the Mount Sion and with Him an hundred forty and four thousand, having His Father's name written in their foreheads. 2. And I heard a voice from heaven as the voice of many waters and as the voice of a great thunder; and I heard the voice of harpers harping with their harps; 3. and they sung as it were a new song before the throne and before the four living ones and the elders; and no man could learn that song but the hundred and forty and four thousand, which were redeemed from the earth. 4. These are they which were not defiled with women; for they are virgins. These are they which follow the Lamb whithersoever He goeth. These were redeemed from among men, being the first fruits unto God and to the Lamb. 5. And in their mouth was found no guile; for they are without fault before the throne of God. 6. And I saw another angel fly in the midst of heaven, having the everlasting Gospel to preach unto them that dwell on the earth, and to every nation and kindred and tongue and people, 7. saying with a loud voice: Fear God, and give glory to Him; for the hour of His judgment is come; and worship Him that made heaven and earth and the sea and the fountains of waters. 8. And there followed another angel, saying: Babylon is fallen, is fallen, that great city, because she made all nations drink of the wine of the wrath of her fornication. 9. And the third angel followed them, saying with a loud voice: If any man worship the beast and his image, and receive his mark in his forehead or in his hand, 10. the same shall drink of the wine of the wrath of God, which is poured out without mixture into the cup of His indignation; and he shall be tormented with fire and brimstone in the presence of the holy angels and in the presence of the Lamb: 11. and the smoke of their torment ascendeth up forever and ever; and they have no rest day nor night who worship the beast and his image, and whosoever receiveth the mark of his name. 12. Here is the patience of the saints; here are they that keep the Commandments of God and the faith of Jesus. 13. And I heard a voice from heaven saying unto me: Write: Blessed are the dead which die in the Lord from henceforth; yea, saith the Spirit, that they may rest from their labors; and their works do follow them. 14. And I looked, and, behold, a white cloud, and upon the cloud One sat like

unto the Son of Man, having on His head a golden crown and in His hand a sharp sickle. 15. And another angel came out of the temple, crying with a loud voice to Him that sat on the cloud: Thrust in Thy sickle and reap; for the time is come for Thee to reap; for the harvest of the earth is ripe. 16. And He that sat on the cloud thrust in His sickle on the earth; and the earth was reaped. 17. And another angel came out of the temple which is in heaven, he also having a sharp sickle. 18. And another angel came out from the altar, which had power over fire, and cried with a loud cry to him that had the sharp sickle, saying: Thrust in thy sharp sickle, and gather the clusters of the vine of the earth; for her grapes are fully ripe. 19. And the angel thrust in his sickle into the earth and gathered the vine of the earth and cast it into the great winepress of the wrath of God. 20. And the winepress was trodden without the city, and blood came out of the winepress, even unto the horse bridles, by the space of a thousand and six hundred furlongs.

This chapter is usually divided into seven visions; but, as the same opening words in vv. 6 and 14 show, it is more properly divided into three visions. These three visions complete the two beast visions already described. The three pictures that appear in the present chapter are pictures of Zion, of Babylon, and of the sickles. The first of these has to do with the fate of the woman who symbolizes the Church (cf. 12:1). The second deals with the vision of the dragon (cf. 12:3). The third, that of the sickles, deals with both the preceding visions and describes the goal of each.

The opening words of v. 1 indicate a distinct vision that was given to John to see, and that not an ordinary vision, but a vision of special significance and importance. What John saw here was "the Lamb." This was not a mere ordinary lamb, but the same Lamb mentioned in v. 6, "the Lamb that had been slain," "the Lamb of God, which taketh away the sin of the world." He saw Him "standing," and thus ready for action, "on Mount Zion."

This Mount Zion is not to be understood literally, but symbolically as a designation of heaven itself (cf. Is. 27:13; Ps. 2:6; Heb. 12:22-24). John saw with the Lamb 144,000 with His name and the name of His Father written on their foreheads. This is the same number mentioned in Chapter 7, and stands here, as there, for the whole number of God's people, the totality of the elect, or the one holy Christian Church. It is notable that he sees them with Jesus Christ, their Redeemer, their Savior, and their Lord. They are with Him on Mount Zion, i. e., in heaven, where they are "forever with the Lord." With the names of the Lamb and of the Father inscribed on their foreheads, they are sealed as God's possession, His very own.

The scene depicted in v. 2 is in heaven, not on earth. It is the voice of the Church Triumphant in its eternal state of blessedness and glory. The voice, which John here declares he heard, is not the voice of a heavenly being, or of an angel; but, as the words that follow show, the voice of the 144,000 themselves. So immense is the volume of this voice proceeding from the whole host of the saved in fervent adoration and glorification of the Lamb, who redeemed them, that it is compared by John to the sound of many waters and to the sound of mighty thunder, as it resounds out of heaven in his ears. In his further description in this verse he gives expression to the melodiousness of this voice, comparing it to the charming melody of harpers who play skillfully on their harps. Heavenly music is entrancing beyond our highest conception!

In the next verse John gives a brief account of the song which he heard. He calls it "new" because it was a song never heard before and because it was a song that could be sung only by the 144,000 redeemed as they give voice to their unique experience as "those that have been bought from the earth." For the content of this song, see 15:3-4. That this song occurs before the throne and before the four living ones and before the elders, indicates their salvation as coming from God's dominion and from His providence and from the ministry of the Word which is ever active in bestowing salvation upon them. In the last clause of this verse it is declared that this song is a song which only the redeemed, the 144,000, who have had the experience that it commemorates, can sing. These are they who, having been bought by the precious blood of Jesus, have in steadfast faith appropriated His redemption and are now in His Kingdom of Glory (cf. 1 Cor. 6:20; 7:23).

These are still further described in v. 4 in symbolical language as "they who were not defiled with women." The fact that the term "these" at the beginning of this verse includes the entire Christian Church, the whole body of believers, shows that the reference here is not to be taken literally, or limited to male celibates, but is symbolical. To apply it to a certain class or party is contrary to the symbolical number, 144,000, and is also a reflection upon the divine institution of marriage. Also to limit it to the participants in a fancied millennium is contrary to the whole tenor of Scripture teaching. Physical defilement with pagan women has almost from the beginning of God's revelation been a symbol of apostasy from God (Gen. 6:5); and so is it used here. In confirmation of the statement in this verse it is added: "for they are virgins." This means to say that they have been preserved in their virginal purity. In the next sentence where they are described as "following the Lamb whithersoever He goeth" the reference is again to the 144,000, or the whole number of the saved without exception (cf. John 10:27). The following of the Lamb is in direct antithesis to the following of the two beasts described in Chapter 13. All who belong to the one holy Christian Church and who in this life followed the Lord Jesus Christ unto the end of their earthly career will follow the Lamb wherever He goes. The sentence that follows shows how they attained the position they now enjoy. This is so because they "were redeemed from among men," i. e., from the earth dwellers, and as such are "first fruits unto God and to the Lamb." Thus they are marked as the Triune God's own possession.

The next verse gives the final description of all the saved. Here it is definitely stated that in their mouth was found no guile, or lie. The word in the original Greek includes anything and everything pertaining to falsehood or untruthfulness; but here it bears special reference to the denial of Christ through the deception of the beast, who is described in 13:14 as "deceiving those that dwell on the earth" (cf. 1 John 1:6-10; 2:22; 4:20). Consequently it is added that all followers of the Lamb are without fault, literally without blemish, before the throne of God (cf. Eph. 5:27).

In the succeeding verses, 6-13, the majority of commentators find three visions, each of the three angels representing a separate vision; but this section is a unit, each of these angels announcing the same thing, viz., the Gospel, the everlasting Gospel of salvation, the Gospel that effects the separation of Mount Zion and Babylon.

In v. 6 begins a description of the second vision recorded in this chapter. John here declares that he saw another angel. As no angel has been mentioned in the preceding verses, it has puzzled many commentators that he should call this angel "another angel" in distinction from the two that are to follow. A description of the activity of this angel now follows. He saw this angel flying in midheaven, i. e., beyond the reach of the antichristian world powers symbolized by the beasts previously described. John sees this angel flying in mid-

heaven having a message to proclaim. This message is
from above, from God, and with it no antichristian powers
can interfere. This message is nothing less than the
"everlasting Gospel," the contents of which are given in
v. 7. In the present verse the character of this message
is emphasized by the use of the same word in the original
Greek as the message of good news. Some authors have
taken the word "angel" here as symbolical and have interpreted this vision as referring to Luther: but, as we have
already noted, the term "angel" is never used symbolically
in the Apocalypse, although it is occasionally used in its
original sense as "messenger." But, while Luther did indeed preach the pure Gospel and set it upon its golden
candlestick in the Church again, he is not to be identified
with this angel who is the messenger from heaven for
the whole New Testament dispensation. His work is not
to be restricted to Luther or the Reformation period, but
includes the proclamation of the blessed Gospel message
through all time. This Gospel is here called "everlasting,"
or "eternal," because it is unchangeable, being forever the
same. The fact that this angel has this eternal Gospel to
proclaim "to those that sit on the earth, and to every nation and tribe and tongue and people," designates it as
a universal Gospel, a Gospel that is to be preached to
every creature. Here we have a fulfillment of Christ's
own prediction in Matt. 24:14. This is a fulfillment which
the devil and all his hosts of darkness cannot prevent.

In v. 7, which immediately follows, we have the contents of this angel's message. He is here described as
speaking with a loud voice, because his message of grace
is the eternal Gospel, with its call to repentance and conversion, which is to be carried to all the inhabitants of
the earth. First of all this angel calls upon all men to
render unto God the reverential awe that is His due from
all His intelligent creatures. In this message there is

clearly set forth the love of God, "who is not willing that any should perish, but that all should come to repentance and be saved." It is also a call to all the inhabitants of the earth to give to God the glory that is due unto His holy name. As an incentive to obey the command just given this angel brings to the front God's judging of men, declaring that this hour of judgment has now arrived. Redemption having been completed, judging is the only work that remains to be done. The reference in this is not limited to the last days, or to the general Judgment at the end of the world; but is God's judgment that came with the exaltation of Christ, the enthronement of the woman's Son (12:5). As proof that the hour of God's judgment has come, see John 3:18; 16:11. It is clear, therefore, that God's judgment has begun and is in progress and will reach its final culmination at the Last Day. But until this culmination is reached, the gracious Gospel call goes forth to fear God and give Him glory. The climax of this angel's gracious Gospel message lies in the call to worship God, reminding us of the Lord's own words in Matt. 4:10: "Thou shalt worship the Lord, thy God, and Him only shalt thou serve" — an obligation binding eternally upon all men, who owe their creation and their redemption to the Lord, their God. Notable here is the description of God as the Maker of heaven and earth and the sea and the fountains of waters. To Him who created all these things judging rightfully belongs. In the works of creation mentioned God revealed His glory. All His judgments that go over creation and use its elements as work tools should direct the eyes of every man's conscience to the Creator, whose last voice of loving admonition, calling men to conversion and repentance, is clearly heard in the Gospel message of the angel in this verse. We surely should take it to heart and seriously and earnestly meditate upon it. "Behold, now is the acceptable time; behold, now is the day of salvation" (2 Cor. 6:2).

In v. 8 we meet with another angel following the first and so, like him, flying in midheaven, expressly designated in the best manuscripts as "a second angel." This angel, like the first, has also a message to proclaim. His message, however, unlike that of the first angel, is a message of judgment. This judgment message is pronounced upon those who will not heed, but who reject the gracious Gospel message brought to them by the first angel. The heart of the message brought by this second angel is the tragic and emphatic proclamation of the final fall and complete destruction of the concentrated power of all opposition to God and His gracious Gospel of life and salvation. This power, here personified as "Babylon the Great," symbolizes the antichristian world city or empire built up by the two beasts described in Chapter 13. This antichristian world, built up with so great zeal and labor by the two beasts, has come to irrevocable destruction. Its ruin is irremediable. Mount Zion, the holy city of God with the Lamb and the 144,000, abides henceforth forever with no hostile Babylon existing to trouble it any more. It is a serious mistake to take Babylon as a symbol for Rome, as is done by many commentators. Such reference fails completely, as this Babylon embraces the whole world. From of old, Babylon has been a symbol of human greatness in antithesis to divine glory. It is employed here in opposition to Zion, the city of God. This Babylon is the antichristian city or empire built up by the two beasts and the demons from the abyss, exerting its evil power in all fields of human culture and authority, paving the way for the glorification of humanity as over against God, and thus leaving no room for Christianity and sentencing it to death. The clause that now follows describes the work that this Babylon has been accomplishing through the ages among all the nations of the world. The expression "fornication," or "whoring," is an expression frequently used in the Old Testament to designate unfaithfulness to God and apostasy from Him. This imagery occurs also in the New Testament and is the imagery employed in these visions. The Greek word here translated "wrath" in our English versions is scarcely suitable. A better translation is "passion," the original meaning of the word. What is intended to be conveyed here is that Babylon with her whoring spirit as the entire antichristian empire throughout the whole New Testament dispensation is assiduously engaged in making men drunk with the passion of her whoring so as to becloud their vision and preclude their seeing God and their belonging to Him. So certain is the doom of this Babylon that it is described here as having already occurred.

In v. 9 a description of a third angel is given. This angel is represented as following the other two, and consequently as also flying in midheaven. Like the first angel, who proclaims the Gospel call, this third angel, who proclaims the Gospel warning, is portrayed as speaking with a loud voice. This is so because the messages of both these angels are to be heard by all the peoples of the world. This was not the case with the second angel, as the fall of Babylon proclaimed in his message occurs as a matter of course and is inevitable. Just as in v. 6 there is presented the positive side of the Gospel, so in this verse is given the negative side. The statement in this vision is a warning of the consequences that will inevitably follow the worshiping of the antichristian power described in Chapter 13. This warning, it should be noted, is not addressed to men in general, but is definitely individualized. Whoever engages in the worship of the beast and his image against which this warning is directed will suffer the consequences so vividly described in the next verse. The first consequence is that every one, whoever he may be, that performs such worship or receives such mark shall drink of the wine of the wrath of God, and that from this consequence there is no possibility of escape. The word here translated "wrath" means "hot anger." This wine of God's wrath, which the offender shall drink, is further defined as "unmixed," and so of full strength. Every such offender shall drink out of the cup of God's unmitigated wrath and anger. Now follows the second consequence that will overtake each and every worshiper of the beast and his image. This is nothing less than that he shall be tormented with fire and brimstone. Fire and brimstone here, as elsewhere in the Scriptures, are descriptive of the torments of hell. These words, whether taken literally or figuratively, signify the most excruciating torments imaginable. In addition to this, these torments are represented as taking place before the holy angels and before the Lamb, which means that both the holy angels and the Lamb acquiesce in the justice and necessity of this display of God's wrath upon those who so richly deserve this punishment. The intensity of this punishment is brought out still more strongly in v. 11, where it is declared that the smoke of their torment goes up forever and ever, or as long as God Himself exists (cf. 1:6). And in order to make this matter clear and to confirm the ceaselessness of this terrible torment, it is added that these worshipers of the beast and his image shall not have a single moment's respite to all eternity. The last clause in this verse takes up and repeats what has just been said in v. 9, in order to show that there will be no exception here; but each and every individual worshiper of the beast and his image will partake of this endless torment.

V. 12 which now follows is not a comment of John upon this vision, but a revelation made to him in connec-

tion with it, which he here records for his readers. The
"patience" mentioned in this verse really means "endurance" (cf. 2:2). The idea here to be conveyed is that the
saints, as they reflect upon the terrible, never-ending
punishment meted out to the wicked, will be moved all
the more readily to endure with patience all the afflictions
that come upon them in this life. Just who these saints
are, is described in the words "they that keep the Commandments of God and the faith of Jesus." Both "Commandments" and "faith" are to be understood objectively
and refer to the same thing, viz., God's revelation in both
Law and Gospel. The Commandments are here ascribed
to God; and the faith, or Gospel of salvation, is referred
to Jesus Christ, the Redeemer (cf. John 1:17).

V. 13 concludes the vision which begins in v. 6. The
voice which John here declares that he heard was not the
voice of an angel, but simply a voice from heaven. As
such it conveys a divine message. As such it contains a
command applicable to all the visions (1.11, 19) and is
found in each of the letters to the seven churches. This
command to John is to write. The specific message which
he is to write is a message of beatitude (cf. the Lord's
Beatitudes, Matt. 5:3-11; also Rev. 1:3). Here, however,
the blessedness is ascribed to the "dead," not indeed to
all the dead, but only to those "that die in the Lord."
The Lord's people, those who in this life lived unto the
Lord, shall in their death die in the Lord. They are not
to forget that with their death life is given unto them.
For them their dying is not judgment, but salvation. They
at their death do not enter into an unknown land, but
pass out of darkness into light. In this respect they stand
out in sharp contrast to those described in the last two
verses, who die apart from the Lord and whose end is
eternal damnation. But who are these dead that die in
the Lord, and in what does their blessedness consist?

They are the whole body of believers, the 144,000 constituting the one holy Christian Church, whose blessedness has just been described in the first verses of this chapter. Dying as true believers, they can never to all eternity lose their blessedness. In what their blessedness consists is disclosed in the promises at the end of each of the letters to the seven churches. St. Paul sums up this blessedness very accurately in, 2 Tim. 4:8. The words "from henceforth" here cover the whole New Testament era from its beginning to its close. An assuring announcement is now given by the Holy Spirit, whose office it is to apply the redemption of Jesus Christ to men, in which is described the negative side of the blessedness of the saints. For all those dying in the Lord, toils are a thing of the past (cf. 7:16-17; 21:4). Explaining this more fully, He assures them that their works wrought in God do not perish, but are preserved and will testify to their faith on the Day of Judgment. Their good works are not to be restricted to such as cause labor and toil and suffering, but are all-inclusive.

The words "And I saw," or "And I looked," v. 14, occur here for the third time in this chapter, each occurrence marking a separate and distinct vision. In this 14th verse we have the Vision of the Two Sickles. There is portrayed here the twofold harvest of the final Judgment — first the harvesting of the godly and then the harvesting of the ungodly (cf. Mark 4:29). The first thing to catch John's attention in this vision is a white cloud. White, as we have seen before, is the symbol of holiness. This white cloud serves as a heavenly throne; and so on this cloud John saw "One sitting like unto the Son of Man." This leaves no doubt as to the Person who here appears. It is none other than Jesus Himself, here assigned the name which He so frequently applies to Himself in the Gospels (cf. also Dan. 7:13). Here the cloud, described

as a "white cloud," stands out in sharp contrast with the
dark cloud of judgment. Jesus comes to His own, not in
judgment, but in grace and glory. He is further described
as wearing on His head a golden crown. Once He wore
a crown of thorns; but now, as He comes to gather His
elect unto Himself, He wears a crown of gold, or in other
words, a crown of glory. The final description of this Son
of Man is that He holds in His hand a sharp sickle —
a symbol of reaping. This sickle He has in His own hand
because this harvest which is to be reaped is His. The
designation of this sickle as "sharp" implies that it will
accomplish its work effectively and completely.

V. 17 introduces the second part of this vision, not on
the same level with the former, but inferior and sec-
ondary. It pictures a judgment of damnation. This "other
angel," like the preceding one (v. 15), came out of the
temple, the seat of God's holiness; and so, like the other,
taking his orders from God. He is also described as having a sharp sickle with which he can swiftly accomplish
his complete and effective work. In the following verse
another angel is described as coming from the altar, thus
designating him also as in the service of God and as
executing God's holy judgment. As coming up out of the
altar and calling to the angel with the sharp sickle to begin the execution of God's judgment, this angel symbolizes the answer to the prayers of the saints (cf. 6:10).
He is further described as having authority over fire. This
fire is the fire burning the incense on the altar, the sweet-
smelling smoke of which goes up to God with the prayers
of the saints. The authority of this angel over the fire has
been given to him by God, and signifies that the time
when final judgment is to be meted out to the wicked is
determined by the will of God in answer to the prayers
of the saints. Just as in v. 15 the command was to send
forth the sharp sickle to reap the grain to gather it into

the heavenly garner in the harvest of the godly, so here
the command given to the angel having the sharp sickle
was to send it forth and gather in the grapes in the great
vine harvest of the ungodly. The time for this action is
fully determined by God, who has set an appointed end
for both the godly and the ungodly as far as this world
is concerned. The wicked are here symbolized under the
figure of "the grape clusters of the vine of the earth." In
Ps. 1:4 and in Matt. 3:12 the wicked are pictured under
the figure of chaff to be burned; here they are likened
to grapes fully ripe. Their wickedness having reached
the limit set by God, the hour of God's judgment upon
them has arrived. Just as in the first part of this vision
the grain was harvested, so here the grape clusters of the
vine are gathered. What follows after this is left to the
disclosure of future visions. By the final expression in this
verse, "for its grapes are fully ripe," the meaning intended
to be conveyed is that the cup of their iniquity is full and
that only the execution of God's righteous wrath remains.

In the next verse is described the action of the angel
in obedience to the command received from the other
angel. This angel is here pictured as thrusting his sickle
into the earth, which accomplished of itself that which it
was intended to do. The result of this action on the part
of the angel was the gathering in of the vine of the earth
and the casting of it into the great winepress of the wrath
of God. This winepress, as symbolizing the wrath of God,
is here graphically described as "great."

The last verse of this chapter discloses the result of the
angel's action. The winepress, immense enough to hold
all the grapes of the world, is declared to be located outside the city. The city here mentioned is neither Jerusalem nor Babylon, but rather the heavenly city, the New
Jerusalem that cometh down from God out of heaven,
from which all that defiles is excluded, as being the object

of God's eternal wrath and torment. In the last chapter of this book (22:15), they are described as being "without," i. e., as forever excluded from fellowship with God and with the blessed. The overwhelming nature of this judgment that crushes the wicked is brought out very emphatically in the last words of this verse, where it is stated that blood came out of the winepress up to the horses' bridles as far as 1,600 furlongs. Inasmuch as four is the number of the world, four times four multiplied by 100 emphasizes its completeness. God's wrath upon the ungodly and His punishment of them could not be more adequately portrayed than is done in this vision. With this chapter the description of the Church Militant closes. In the remaining chapters the Church Triumphant is described, and the state of believers is portrayed as they exist in the Kingdom of Glory.

Chapter 15

1. And I saw another sign in heaven, great and marvelous: seven angels having the seven last plagues; for in them is filled up the wrath of God. 2. And I saw as it were a sea of glass mingled with fire; and them that had gotten the victory over the beast and over his image and over his mark and over the number of his name stand on the sea of glass, having the harps of God. 3. And they sing the song of Moses, the servant of God, and the song of the Lamb, saying: Great and marvelous are Thy works, Lord God Almighty; just and true are Thy ways, Thou King of saints. 4. Who shall not fear Thee, O Lord, and glorify Thy name? For Thou only art holy; for all nations shall come and worship before Thee; for Thy judgments are made manifest. 5. And after that I looked, and behold, the temple of the tabernacle of the testimony in heaven was opened; 6. and the seven angels came out of the temple, having the seven plagues, clothed in pure and white linen, and having their breasts girded with golden girdles. 7. And one of the four

*living ones gave unto the seven angels seven golden vials full of
the wrath of God, who liveth forever and ever. 8. And the temple
was filled with smoke from the glory of God and from His power;
and no man was able to enter into the temple, till the seven plagues
of the seven angels were fulfilled.*

This and the following chapter set forth the
Vision of the Seven Angels with the Seven
Vials, or Bowls, the present chapter being introductory,
and Chapter 16 picturing the seven angels actually pouring out the wrath of God upon the antichristian world
empire as a token of the final judgment, which will overtake and overwhelm it. These preliminary judgments are
God's last warnings to the ungodly.

In the first verse John describes what he saw in this
vision as "another sign," so called because of the two
signs that preceded (12:1, 3). The first of these was that
of the woman, symbolizing the Church. The second was
that of the dragon, the devil, and his two beasts, symbolizing the antichristian power and antichristian propaganda whereby the antichristian world empire, represented by Babylon, is raised up. Now comes the third
sign, in which God is represented as smiting the world
empire with seven plagues before finally and completely
crushing it in the last Judgment. The description of this
sign as "great and wonderful" indicates its importance
and the astonishment which it occasions. By way of explanation he tells in what this great and wonderful sign
consists. It is that of seven angels having the seven last
plagues. Angels are thus employed as God's ministering
servants who do His commands, hearkening unto the
voice of His word (Ps. 103:20). The number seven, here
as elsewhere, is symbolical of God's dealings with men.
The reference in the present case is to God's punitive
dealing with men in sending these plagues. These plagues

are not literally seven in number, but represent God's last punitive judgments that precede the final Judgment. The statement in the last clause of this verse is prophetic, describing as already accomplished that which will be completed when the goal set by God is reached.

In v. 2 John describes more specifically what he saw in this vision. It was a sea that John saw, the same sea described previously in 4:6, where the description of it as mixed with fire and as having people standing upon it is omitted. This sea is symbolical of divine providence. Seen from above, or from God's throne, it is transparent, clear as crystal; but viewed from below, it is full of darkness, mysterious, and impenetrable. The expression here, "mixed with fire," designates it as referring to God's punitive providence symbolized in the preceding verse. John not only saw the sea, but saw the conquerors standing upon it. These he describes as those who came forth victors from the battle with the beast and his image and the number of his name. As standing on the sea, these conquerors are pictured as standing on the sure and solid foundation of God's providence, which constitutes for them an impregnable fortress in which their safety is fully assured. They are further described as having in their hands "harps of God," so called from the Giver of them. God gave them these harps to accompany therewith their song of glory to God (cf. 5:8; 14:2).

In the next two verses the contents of the song of these conquerors is given. It is described as "the song of Moses and the song of the Lamb." This does not mean that it is two songs; but that this song deals with what God wrought through His servant Moses and what He wrought through Christ. The praise given by the Israelites on the shore of the Red Sea and in the Song of Moses is a type of a greater reality. The song of Moses is exalted through the song of the Lamb. Accordingly in the song on the

crystal sea all glory is gathered together, and the time of
beginning is joined with the time of completion. Deliverance through Moses from Egyptian bondage foreshadowed the greater deliverance through Christ from
the beast and his image and his number (cf. Heb. 3:5-6).
In the first stanza of this song, which now follows, an
ascription of praise is assigned to God in the significant
titles "Lord" and "the Almighty" ascribed to Him, and
in designating His works as "great and wonderful" (cf.
Amos 4:13). Such lordship, all, even demoniacal powers,
must serve. Now follows a second strophe of praise in
the words: "righteous and genuine are Thy ways, Thou
King of the nations" (this is the best translation according
to the N. T. manuscripts). This also corresponds with
Moses' song in Deut. 32:4, which reads: "For all His ways
are judgment; a God of truth and without iniquity, just
and right is He." Also the ascription "God of the nations"
finds adequate expression in Ps. 86:9, which declares: "All
nations whom Thou hast made shall come and worship
before Thee, O Lord, and shall glorify Thy name." These
Old Testament passages are here strengthened by adding
the word "only" to give the idea of absoluteness to the
final act of redemption as expressed in such passages as
Rom. 16:27 and 1 Tim. 6:16. That God is righteous in all
His judgments and in all His acts is now known to all
the world.

V. 4 opens with a rhetorical question: "Who shall not
fear Thee, O Lord, and glorify Thy name?" To this question the answer is obvious. Absolutely all without exception must willingly, or unwillingly, fear and glorify the
name of God; and by the name of God is meant the revelation by which men know and can alone know Him
(cf. Phil. 2:10). The reason assigned for this is, because
it is holy, literally sacred, which holiness, or sacredness,
is manifest to all. So evident is God's holiness that all

the nations, whether willingly or unwillingly, shall be obliged to acknowledge it (cf. Phil. 2:10). Why this is so is explained by the fact that God's righteous judgments were made manifest. Scripture constantly affirms that in the end the whole universe shall acknowledge the righteousness of all God's acts and judgments.

V. 5 refers back to what immediately precedes in vv. 2-4, the song pertaining to the last plagues in which the wrath of God is finished. The first impression made upon John in this vision is the temple in heaven opened. The temple, or sanctuary, symbolizes these last plagues as sent from the holiness of God. This imagery is taken from the Tabernacle of Moses rather than from the Temple of Solomon (cf. Acts 7:44). The Tabernacle of Moses testified to God's presence with the Children of Israel during their long journey through the wilderness. It thus becomes an appropriate symbol of the heavenly seat of God's presence for worship on the part of His saints.

In the next verse is described the coming forth out of the opened sanctuary of the seven angels bearing with them the seven plagues. They are here represented as coming from the immediate presence of God's holiness, which holiness will attest itself for the last time in these seven plagues. These angels are described as clothed in linen pure and bright, i. e., in white linen; white being the symbol of holiness. They are so represented as being the agents of God's holiness. Their further description as being girded with golden girdles about their breasts is a reminder of what is said of Christ Himself in 1:13. In both cases the golden girdle symbolizes royalty. These angels are described as thus clothed because they are in the service of the Lord their King.

In v. 7 is described the act of one of the four living ones, the earthly agents of God's providence, in relation to these seven angels, God's heavenly agents. It is quite fitting that one of these should be employed to turn over to the seven angels the execution of the last plagues. The earthly agents having finished their work, place what remains to be done in the hands of the heavenly agents.

In the last verse of this chapter is given a description of the results that followed. Here the temple filled with smoke from the glory of God reminds us of a similar situation in which the Prophet Isaiah found himself when he was sent by God to bring divine judgment to Israel (cf. Is. 6:4-12). It also reminds us of the experience of Moses recorded in Ex. 40:34-35. The result of this filling of the temple with smoke is set forth in the last clause, which declares that no one was able to enter into the temple till these seven plagues should be finished. This is an indication that God's work of grace is over and that all that remains to be done is the sending of the last plagues, which are now on the point of being carried out with the swiftness of divine judgment.

Chapter 16

1. *And I heard a great voice out of the temple saying to the seven angels: Go your ways, and pour out the vials of the wrath of God upon the earth.* 2. *And the first went and poured out his vial upon the earth; and there fell a noisome and grievous sore upon the men which had the mark of the beast and upon them which worshiped his image.* 3. *And the second angel poured out his vial upon the sea; and it became as the blood of a dead man; and every living soul died in the sea.* 4. *And the third angel poured out his vial upon the rivers and fountains of waters; and they became blood.* 5. *And I heard the angel of the waters say: Thou art righteous, O Lord, which art and wast and shalt be, because Thou hast judged thus.* 6. *For they have shed the blood of saints and*

prophets, and Thou hast given them blood to drink; for they are worthy. 7. And I heard another out of the altar say: Even so, Lord God Almighty, true and righteous are Thy judgments. 8. And the fourth angel poured out his vial upon the sun; and power was given unto him to scorch men with fire. 9. And men were scorched with great heat and blasphemed the name of God, which hath power over these plagues; and they repented not to give Him glory. 10. And the fifth angel poured out his vial upon the seat of the beast; and his kingdom was full of darkness; and they gnawed their tongues for pain 11. and blasphemed the God of heaven because of their pains and their sores and repented not of their deeds. 12. And the sixth angel poured out his vial upon the great river Euphrates; and the water thereof was dried up, that the way of the kings of the East might be prepared. 13. And I saw three unclean spirits like frogs come out of the mouth of the dragon and out of the mouth of the beast and out of the mouth of the false prophet. 14. For they are the spirits of devils, working miracles, which go forth unto the kings of the earth and of the whole world to gather them to the battle of that great day of God Almighty. 15. Behold, I come as a thief. Blessed is he that watcheth and keepeth his garments, lest he walk naked and they see his shame. 16. And he gathered them together into a placed called in the Hebrew tongue Armageddon. 17. And the seventh angel poured out his vial into the air; and there came a great voice out of the temple of heaven, from the throne, saying: It is done. 18. And there were voices and thunders and lightnings; and there was a great earthquake, such as was not since men were upon the earth, so mighty an earthquake and so great. 19. And the great city was divided into three parts, and the cities of the nations fell; and great Babylon came in remembrance before God to give unto her the cup of the wine of the fierceness of His wrath. 20. And every island fled away, and the mountains were not found. 21. And there fell upon men a great hail out of heaven, every stone about the weight of a talent; and men blasphemed God because of the plague of the hail; for the plague thereof was exceeding great.

A fitting title for this chapter would be: The Pouring Out of the Seven Bowls. The first verse is introductory to what follows. There again, as frequently before, John heard "a great voice." Whose voice

this was is not definitely stated; but as this voice came out
of the temple, God's holy dwelling place, it is evident that
this voice comes from God. The words of this voice are
addressed to the seven angels collectively, issuing to them
a command to pour out the seven bowls of the wrath of
God upon the earth. This command they, as God's willing
and obedient servants, must obey. This they do, one after
the other, in rapid succession, just as stroke follows stroke,
until the end is reached, as the verses that follow show.
The pouring out of these bowls of plagues is symbolical,
pointing to and preceding the final Judgment to its very
door, although not including it. All attempts to explain
the matter here presented in literal terms are futile, as
such events cannot be located in past history. The language is prophetic and couched in symbolical terms; but
beneath these symbols lie stern realities.

The second verse indicates the prompt obedience of
the first of the seven angels to the command of the voice
out of the temple. While this is said only of the first angel,
it is understood as applying to the others also. It is specifically stated that this first angel did as he was commanded
and poured out his bowl of wrath upon the earth. The
result of this outpouring, which immediately followed, is
described as a bad and evil sore or ulcer, indicating its
extremely vicious painfulness. This sore, it is further
stated, came upon all those human beings without exception who had the mark of the beast and worshiped his
image. While this is stated only of the first plague, it
applies to all the rest as well. None of these plagues, however, touched any of those who did not bear the mark of
the beast or worship his image. Just as the Children of
Israel were spared in the Egyptian plagues, so those who
bear the seal of the Lord as belonging to Him are spared
from this plague. It is absurd, however, to take this sore
to mean a literal physical ulcer with which all antichris-

tians will be afflicted previous to the Lord's second coming. Those upon whom this plague will be visited are the worshipers of the beast, the "earth dwellers," or "Babylon" — the whole antichristian multitude on earth "out of every tribe and people and tongue and nation" (13:7), "the small and the great, the rich and the poor, the free and the slave" (13:16). Under this sore, or ulcer, are embraced all the disorders in all the various spheres of human activity found wherever the antichristian power holds sway. The picture thus portrayed gives an inkling of the severity with which God in His providence will smite all the followers of the beast. This is the first and the smallest of the plagues with which they will be smitten. The others follow in increasing severity.

In v. 3 we are given a picture of the second angel pouring out his bowl, not upon the earth, but into the sea, with still direr consequences to the followers of the beast. The sea is probably mentioned here as being more susceptible to the imagery that follows. The result which immediately followed the outpouring of this second bowl is now described. The whole sea was turned into blood, and that, not pure, fresh, living, or running blood, but blood like that of a dead person, putrid, foul, malodorous, and vile in the extreme, spreading its deadly odor over the whole world. The outpouring of the first bowl produced virulent ulcers on the followers of the beast. The outpouring of the second bowl had still worse consequences, overwhelming them with death and enveloping them with a stench of rotting, coagulated blood so terrible that it can be adequately described only by the picture of the whole ocean reeking with rotten blood. The whole antichristian world is here pictured as doomed and as reeking with the smell of death. But neither the outpouring of this bowl nor that of any of the others affects the followers of the Lamb.

The outpouring of the third bowl by the third angel is described in v. 4. This angel poured out his bowl upon the fresh waters — the streams and the springs — which sustain the lives of men and which they must have to drink. This plague is still more severe than the preceding one. By the changing of all drinking water into blood, men are deprived of that which is absolutely necessary to their existence. This expression, however, is not to be taken literally, as in such case it would affect alike both the godly and the ungodly. It is used here symbolically to denote the complete corruption of all the sources of natural human wisdom, knowledge, and sound understanding, from which men must draw in all the various departments of life. These waters are indeed already contaminated and polluted under God's restrained anger; but when all restraint has been removed and God's wrath bursts forth in all its fullness, the corruption of these waters will be complete. This third bowl is more drastic still than the other two and exemplifies the Scripture truth that it is "a fearful thing to fall into the hands of the living God" and thus to incur the judgment of His righteous wrath.

In v. 5 are quoted the words of this third angel, here called "the angel of the waters," praising God and commending Him for His righteous judgment which he as His ministering servant has just carried out. He describes God as the eternally existing One, as the Holy, or Sacred One (15:4), who cannot do otherwise than maintain holiness, or sanctity, against all who would presume or attempt to befoul it. God's judgment here is fitting proof, full evidence of the attributes just ascribed to Him. It is impossible for such a One to do otherwise than to judge righteously.

V. 6, which follows, presents conclusive proof that God did judge righteously in this case. Because these followers of the beast had poured out the blood of saints and prophets, God gave them blood to drink. It is pure justice on God's part that, instead of the pure water which they formerly had, these murderers of God's saints and prophets should be given blood to drink. The last words of this verse, "they are worthy," show conclusively that these antichristian forces have fully merited the judgment visited upon them by God in His righteous wrath.

Further commendation of God's judgings is given in v. 7. According to the best manuscripts the opening words of this verse read: "And I heard the altar saying." This expression appears to personify the altar; but this is only apparent. In view of what has been said in 14:18, it is the angel from the altar rather than the altar itself that John heard speaking. The announcement of the angel now follows. It is similar in its expression to that of the angel of the waters in v. 5 and is a full confirmation of it. Here God is first addressed as the Almighty (cf. 1:8; 11:17; 15:3). Then His judgings are declared to be genuine, i. e., without pretense or sham, and righteous (cf. v. 5). God is again described by this angel as meeting out righteous judgment in giving blood to drink to these bloodthirsty followers of the beast.

In v. 8 the fourth angel is portrayed as pouring out his bowl upon the sun. This vision symbolizes a plague more severe and more torturing than any of the preceding visions. The physical sun giving forth normal heat and light is warming and cheering; but, turned into fire and scorching heat, it is torturing. This presents to us a picture of all that makes life comfortable turned into intolerable burning and poured out unceasingly upon the enemies of God and the Lamb. This plague also does not touch those who have the seal of God upon them, to whom the Lord God is a sun and shield and upon whom "the Sun of Righteousness shall arise with healing in His

wings" (Ps. 84:11; Mal. 4:2). The function of the sun is
indicated in the last words of this verse: "and it was given
to it," i. e., to the sun, "to scorch human beings with fire."
This, of course, was done by God, in whose service this
angel stands.

In the next verse the effect of this pouring out by the
angel of his bowl upon the sun is set forth. The earth
dwellers, upon whom it was outpoured, were burned with
a great burning. Their reaction is next described. Far
from repenting of their sins which had brought this judgment upon them, they blasphemed God, who had authority over these plagues and who had sent this plague upon
them.

V. 10 describes the act of the fifth angel in pouring out
his bowl upon the seat, i. e., the throne of the beast. The
word "throne" stands for power, rule, and dominion,
which proceed from the dragon (13:2). The throne of
the beast and the dragon, set up in opposition to the
throne of God, is now smitten by the wrath of God poured
out upon it by this fifth angel. The result was a permanent
darkening of the kingdom of the beast. A dark pall of
doom settled over his entire kingdom, which had been
built up by means of his throne. This kingdom includes
all the earth dwellers — followers and worshipers of the
beast. The effect of the outpouring of this bowl of God's
wrath upon the victims was the producing of such torture
and anguish as can only be adequately described as "the
gnawing of their tongues from pain."

In v. 11 their reaction is set forth. It called forth from
them only blasphemy against the God of heaven, who had
blasted them with His judgment of darkness and had
brought upon them such excruciating pain and such horrible ulcers or sores. But these judgments of God, far
from bringing them to repent of their evil works, served
only to provoke them to still greater rage against Him.

Note here again, God is not called "their God," but "the God of heaven."

In v. 12 the sixth angel is presented as pouring out his bowl upon the Euphrates. This river has been mentioned before in connection with the trumpet visions (9:14). There it is described, just as is done here, as "the great river." In both instances the name is used not in a geographical, but in a symbolical sense, and stands for the antichristian world power, or dominion. Just as in 9:13 we have a picture of supernatural judgment in the form of delusion, so here we have the curse of delusion in still more accentuated form in the preparation for the last battle of all the antichristian powers, which results in their utter defeat and final overthrow. The effect of the outpouring of the sixth angel's bowl was the drying up of the water of this river; and God's purpose in this was to make ready the way for these antichristian powers to gather themselves together for the great battle that is to issue in their final and everlasting doom. God in His wrath prepares the road for them. These kings from the sunrising symbolize the great gathering of the antichristian powers for the great battle against God.

V. 13 stands in close connection with the preceding verse and adds some special features to what has already been said concerning the antichristian powers represented by the kings from the sunrising. What John saw here was three unclean spirits like frogs coming, one out of the mouth of the dragon, i. e., of Satan (12:9); one out of the mouth of the beast, i. e., the antichristian world power (13:1); and one out of the mouth of the false prophet, i. e., the antichristian world propaganda (the second beast, 13:11). That this false prophet is the second beast is quite clear from the description of him in 13:14. What proceeds out of the mouths of these three demoniacal powers is indicated in the words: "three unclean spirits, as it were frogs." This passage speaks of demoniacal beings born in the deepest filth of hell, who cover and permeate all human thinking with the hellish spew of devilish mania. These unclean spirits are pictured under the imagery of vile, horrible frogs which come from the trinity of evil — a caricature of the Holy Trinity.

In the following verse John explains what is implied in the imagery of "three unclean spirits like frogs." These are spirits of demons. They are further described as active, "doing signs," which, though they are lying signs (13:14), are nevertheless impressive and convincing to the followers of the beast. They are pictured here as going forth to the kings of the whole inhabited world, before whom they perform their signs, by means of which they draw their allegiance to the prince of this world, the master whom they serve. Their purpose in this is to gather together all the antichristian forces of the world into a single vast army for battle against the Almighty. This is described as "the battle of the great day of God the Almighty," for the supreme battle for which God Himself has prepared the way. These antichristian forces willingly unite for this battle, imagining that this is their day and that they will come forth victorious in the battle against the kingdom of God and His Christ and that their might is invincible. "But He that sitteth in the heavens shall laugh; the Lord shall have them in derision" (Ps. 2:4).

V. 15 contains a beatitude, the words of which are not the words of John, as some commentators suppose, but are the words of the Lord Jesus Christ Himself (cf. 3:3; Matt. 24:43; 1 Thess. 5:2; 2 Peter 3:10). The reference in the first sentence is to Christ's second coming in power and great glory for judgment, which coming will be sudden and unexpected and will take the world of earth dwellers totally unawares. The second sentence combines both a beatitude and a warning. He is pronounced blessed who heeds the Lord's admonition to watch and who is constantly looking for his Lord's appearing and is keeping his garments, "lest he walk naked and they see his shame." This admonition is evidently an allusion to 3:18, where Christ exhorts the Laodiceans to buy of Him "white garments that they may be clothed and that the shame of their nakedness may not appear." These white garments symbolize Christ's righteousness, which hides the disgraceful nakedness of our sins, which otherwise would be exposed to the sight of all eyes. This is certainly a beatitude that should be taken to heart by us all.

V. 16 gives an account of the gathering together of the antichristian powers for the great battle against Almighty God. The subject here is without doubt the three unclean spirits just described as like frogs. The battle itself is not here described; but the name of the place of this gathering together is given in the Hebrew as Armageddon. This does not denote a geographical location, but refers to the great battlefield against all the forces of evil in which will occur their final and utter defeat. This battle on the divine side is described in 19:11 ff.

In v. 17 is given a description of the pouring out by the seventh angel of his bowl into the air. The first angel poured out his bowl into the earth; the second into the sea; the third into the rivers and fountains of waters; the fourth into the sun; and now the seventh angel into the air. This appears to be the sequence, the fifth and sixth bowls being exceptions. This pouring out of God's wrath into the air is not to be understood as poisoning the air, but rather as producing convulsions in the air and on the earth. It, like the others, affects only the earth dwellers, or the antichristian empire typified by Babylon the Great (v. 19). This antichristian empire embraces all opposition to God, whether coming from the papacy at Rome, or from Mohammedanism, or from Judaism, or from Unitarianism, or from Modernism, or from Sectarianism, or any other source. The pouring out of this seventh bowl brings us very near to the final Judgment. It sets all the forces of the atmosphere and the earth itself in catastrophic commotion. In the outpouring of this final bowl of wrath, God is no longer represented as being at a distance, but as immediately near at hand. The first occurrence following the outpouring of this bowl is now given. A voice is heard, and that not an ordinary voice, but "a great voice" coming out of the temple from the throne. As coming from this source, this voice is to be regarded as none other than the voice of God Himself. The announcement of this voice finds expression in the words "It is done," or better translated, "It hath occurred." In other words, God's wrath has now been poured out in all its fullness and finality.

The next verse vividly depicts the commotions that immediately followed the announcement just given. These are described as voices and thunders and lightnings and a mighty earthquake. The voices here are not the voices of human beings or angels or other heavenly beings; but are like the sounds or noises of the lightnings and the thunders (cf. 1 Cor. 14:10). And the earthquake, described as great and mighty such as men on earth had never experienced before, symbolizes the complete and overwhelming destruction of the antichristian empire. No wonder it is described at the close of this verse: "So mighty an earthquake, so great!" The result of these terrible commotions is described in v. 19. The first statement here is that the great city, i. e., Babylon, the antichristian world city or empire, was divided into three parts. This implies that the whole city has fallen into utter ruin with the collapse of every structure in it, one wall falling to the right and the opposite wall to the left, the roof structure falling between them. Thus proud Babylon, hitherto regarded as so strong, has now become a heap of ruins. The next reference in this verse is to the vassal cities of this noted capital of the great antichristian empire. These all likewise fell. The antichristian propaganda in all its various forms may erect great, strong, and mighty cities; but one doom awaits them all, the doom of utter destruction which will be visited upon them in the day of God's righteous judgment. Next we are told why the destruction just mentioned was visited upon this great city. This was because Babylon with all that she stood for came into remembrance before God "to give to her the cup of the wine of the anger of His wrath." The duplication of these terms describing God's wrath designates it as poured out in the highest degree in all its fullness. God's long-suffering and patience with the wicked, giving them space for repentance and allowing them to fill up the measure of their iniquity, appears like forgetfulness on His part; but God's overlooking of iniquity will not last forever. The time will eventually arrive when God will remember in righteous judgment to punish the guilty and inflict upon them the whole furor of His wrath. Retribution may be long delayed, but will eventually be meted out without restraint.

V. 20 begins the description of the utter destruction that befell as a result of God's punitive justice. So devastating was it that neither island however remote or insignificant, nor mountain however great or formidable, escaped God's resistless wrath. Islands and mountains stand here as symbols of all earthly exaltation and greatness, exhibited everywhere and at all times by the antichristian empire. All human fortresses and places of ref-

uge flee before God's judgment of wrath and are no more
to be found. This description continues in v. 21. Here it
is great hail coming down from God out of heaven upon
human beings. This corresponds closely with the description given in v. 17. All these destructive powers form a
unit coming down from God out of heaven. This hail, like
the earthquake previously described, was inconceivably
great. It was of unheard-of dimensions, its size being the
weight of a talent, from 60 to 100 lbs. of our measure.
This symbolizes the great and inconceivably destructive
power. This is visited upon human beings, viz., the earth
dwellers. The effect of this hail upon those who survived
it is the same as in all previous cases of God's catastrophic
judgments. Human beings, instead of being brought to
repentance by these judgments are angered and embit-
tered by them. They give vent to their hatred in blasphemy against God, who is the source of this plague, and
all the more so because it was so exceeding great. This is
the climax of the outpouring of the seven bowls, symbolizing in a cumulative way the destruction of the whole antichristian empire. The picture closes with a delineation of
human beings still raging in blasphemy against God — an
implication that further visions are to come which will
exhibit God's last and final dealings with them.

Chapter 17

---

1. *And there came one of the seven angels which had the seven
vials, and talked with me, saying unto me: Come hither; I will show
unto thee the judgment of the great whore that sitteth upon many
waters, 2. with whom the kings of the earth have committed fornication, and the inhabitants of the earth have been made drunk*

with the wine of her fornication. 3. So he carried me away in the spirit into the wilderness. And I saw a woman sit upon a scarlet-colored beast, full of names of blasphemy, having seven heads and ten horns. 4. And the woman was arrayed in purple and scarlet color and decked with gold and precious stones and pearls, having a golden cup in her hand full of abominations and filthiness of her fornication; 5. and upon her forehead was a name written: MYSTERY, BABYLON THE GREAT, THE MOTHER OF HARLOTS AND ABOMINATIONS OF THE EARTH. 6. And I saw the woman drunken with the blood of the saints and with the blood of the martyrs of Jesus; and when I saw her, I wondered with great admiration. 7. And the angel said unto me: Wherefore didst thou marvel? I will tell thee the mystery of the woman and of the beast that carrieth her, which hath the seven heads and ten horns. 8. The beast that thou sawest was and is not; and shall ascend out of the bottomless pit and go into perdition: and they that dwell on the earth shall wonder, whose names were not written in the Book of Life from the foundation of the world, when they behold the beast that was and is not and yet is. 9. And here is the mind which hath wisdom. The seven heads are seven mountains, on which the woman sitteth. 10. And there are seven kings; five are fallen, and one is, and the other is not yet come; and when he cometh, he must continue a short space. 11. And the beast that was and is not, even he is the eighth, and is of the seven, and goeth into perdition. 12. And the ten horns which thou sawest are ten kings, which have received no kingdom as yet, but receive power as kings one hour with the beast. 13. These have one mind and shall give their power and strength unto the beast. 14. These shall make war with the Lamb, and the Lamb shall overcome them; for He is Lord of Lords and King of Kings; and they that are with Him are called and chosen and faithful. 15. And he saith unto me: The waters which thou sawest, where the whore sitteth, are peoples and multitudes and nations and tongues. 16. And the ten horns which thou sawest upon the beast, these shall hate the whore and shall make her desolate and naked and shall eat her flesh and burn her with fire. 17. For God hath put in their hearts to fulfill His will and to agree and give their kingdom unto the beast, until the words of God shall be fulfilled. 18. And the woman which thou sawest is that great city which reigneth over the kings of the earth.

This chapter together with Chapter 18 and vv. 1-10 of Chapter 19 deals with the Great Whore, Babylon, or the antichristian empire,* presenting her to us in all her seductiveness. In the present chapter a picture of this Great Whore is given, and her history is related. In Chapter 18 her glory is exhibited, and the great lamentation over her fall is described. In Chapter 19 praise is rendered unto God for the judgment which He has visited upon her. The picture is here set before us in all its vividness.

In the first verse the messenger that came and spoke to John is definitely designated as one of the seven angels having the bowls. It is useless to speculate as to which one of the seven angels this was, as all of these angels (15:6) came out of the temple. The words "talked with me" imply a friendly conversation. The first words of this angel are an invitation to John to come into his presence in order to show him the judgment that is meted out on the great whore. Why she is called the great whore and further described as sitting upon many waters, is made clear in what follows (see vv. 2, 15). Her sitting upon many waters is a symbol of her established rule (cf. 4:2).

In v. 2 the title "the great whore," given in v. 1, is justified. The supremacy of this whore is evidenced by the fact that all the kings of the earth have become her paramours. Whoredom is one of the most frequently recurring images in the Old Testament for apostasy from God by turning to the vile and filthy abominations of the heathen. This imagery reaches its climax in the description of this whore in v. 5 as "the great one" and as "the mother of the whores." In the second clause of this verse the effect of this whore's influence upon the earth dwellers

---

* Many Lutheran commentators interpret the "mother of harlots" to be the Antichrist and not all anti-Christian forces.

is depicted in their being made drunk from the wine of her whoring (cf. 14:8 for a similar situation). The combination here of drunkenness and whoredom intensifies the idea of moral depravity and filthiness for which each of these words stand. This whoredom includes in its scope all those whose names are not written in the Lamb's Book of Life, all the worshipers of the beast, or in a word, the antichristian powers (cf. v. 15). This is in full accord with the preceding symbols leading up to this one (cf. 13:1-10, 11-18; 14:8; 16:12-16). Here under the image of the great whore, Babylon the Great appears again, now clothed with all antichristian seductiveness, luring the earth dwellers to commit whoredom with her and making them drunk with the wine of her whoring. The kings mentioned in this connection are not individual kings, whether ancient or modern, but are so called as ruling over the various domains of the earth life that is characterized by antagonistic opposition to God and His kingdom. The earth dwellers are the antichristian multitudes who follow the kings as their leaders in their infatuation with the whore and who are carried away by her seductions. This is presented here as already having taken place.

In v. 3 John declares that the angel now bore him in spirit away into a desert, i. e., into a lonely place far away from and uncontaminated by the earth dwellers. From this place he is to have a clear view of the whore, the representative of antichristian seduction. What John saw here in vision was "a woman sitting on a scarlet-colored beast filled with names of blasphemy." This beast is the first beast, described in Chapter 14, and symbolizes the whole antichristian power. The woman symbolizes the whole antichristian seduction; and as sitting upon the beast, she is represented as exercising the power of the beast in carrying out her seduction. She is dependent upon the beast that carries her. The beast is further described as filled with names of blasphemy and as having seven heads and ten horns (cf. 13:1). Accordingly the beast is described as "scarlet." Scarlet, the opposite of white, is the color of sin. It thus designates this beast as belonging to the kingdom of darkness, or hell. The relationship between the whore and the beast and their close connection with each other are well brought out in this verse.

V. 4 now gives a clear picture of this woman in all her seductiveness. She is described here as clothed in the attractive raiment of a queen, whereby she impressed the kings over whom she rules, and drew them to herself. Her purple and scarlet correspond to the scarlet color of the beast. She is further described as "decked with gold and precious stones and pearls" — an exceedingly rich adornment wherewith to impress and allure. In addition to this, she is pictured as holding in her hand a golden cup as an attractive enticement to drink of its contents. This cup is described as "full of abominations," explained as consisting of "the unclean things of her whoring." Here are described in a very vivid way all the attractive seductions in every sphere of life that are abominable in the sight of God, but which the antichristian seduction serves up to the earth dwellers, its devotees, who eagerly swallow its contents.

In v. 5 the woman is described as having a name written on her forehead. The name "Mystery" here applied to her is descriptive and is intended to reveal the true nature of this woman. Mystery is a designation of that which is hidden; but it does not imply that it is to remain hidden. Frequently it points to something that is about to be revealed. Such revelation is made both with respect to the woman and with respect to the beast in v. 7. The great whore here so graphically described is none other than Babylon the Great (cf. 14:8; 16:19). An advance over previous descriptions is made in this verse in the designation of her as "the mother of whores and of the abominations of the earth." This characterizes her as the Supreme Antichristian Seductress, the mother of all whores, and the source of all the antichristian abominations of the earth. The whores of which she is the mother are "the kings of the earth" (16:14). The abominations are the contents of the golden cup, i. e., all the attractive seductions abominable in the sight of God, which she serves to her dupes in every sphere of life.

In v. 6, where this woman is described as drunken from the blood of the saints and from the blood of the witnesses of Jesus, the bloodthirstiness of this whore in her nefarious activity is strongly set forth. This receives confirmation again in 18:24. John expresses marvelous wonder over this vision which had been given him to see. John's wonder was called forth by the sight of this woman, the antichristian Babylon, the great whore and mother of whores, from whom come all of the seductions by which men are enticed into the ranks of all the antichristian forces that are found in the world. This woman is not represented here as an adulteress who is unfaithful to her husband, but as a whore who never had a husband. Consequently the symbolism is not limited to the degenerate Church or the Papacy, although these are included as part of the antichristianity that takes in the whole wide world and manifests itself in all the various forms of opposition to God. Babylon, Tyre, Rome, and many modern cities may be regarded as partial manifestations, but this great Babylon transcends them all.

In the following verse the same angel that spoke to John in v. 1 speaks to him again. Now he inquires of him the reason for his wondering. This he does, not as finding fault with him for it, but as preparatory to give answer

to the questions that arose in John's mind. Without delay
the angel assures John that he will tell him "the mystery
of the woman and of the beast that carrieth her." These
two, as we have frequently seen before, belong together
and are closely connected. Antichristian seduction re-
quires the antichristian power in order to accomplish its
work effectively throughout the wide world among all
nations, tribes, peoples, and tongues. The name "Mystery" used in v. 5 is here assigned both to the woman and
to the beast. The beast is here described as having seven
heads and ten horns, precisely as is done in v. 3. The
significance of these heads and horns is explained in what
follows, particularly in v. 9. A description of this beast
follows in v. 8. The beast is the same beast described by
John in 13:1 ff. To the description previously given is
added that this beast "was, and is not, and is about to
come up out of the abyss." And this is repeated again
with slight variation at the close of this verse. This mysterious expression has been variously understood; but the
only proper explanation is that involved in the expressions
here used. The assertion that this beast "was" means that
he existed previously to his coming up out of the sea
(13:1). In the words "and is not" the reference is to the
deathblow inflicted upon him by the exaltation of Christ,
whereby he was so completely crushed that he was
thrown into the abyss, from which it seemed that he
would never rise again. But according to 13:3-4 his
deadly wound was healed through the power of Satan.
The last expression, "and is about to come up out of the
abyss," inasmuch as the only abyss known in the Scriptures is hell, the reference here is to the second coming
up of the beast after his deadly wound was healed, and
not to his first coming up mentioned in 13:1. The added
expression, "and goeth into perdition," means that he
goeth into "the lake of fire and brimstone" (cf. 19:20;

20:10). The effect upon the earth dwellers, whose names
are not recorded in the Book of Life from the foundation
of the world, when they saw the beast returning after his
deadly wound was healed, was amazing admiration. They
imagined that his power was invincible and that nothing
could ever conquer the antichristian power, which this
beast symbolizes (cf. 13:4 ff.).

V. 9 opens with an introduction to what the angel has
to say about the heads and the horns of this beast. This
is somewhat similar in its expression to the introduction
to the number of the beast in 13:18. "The mind which
hath wisdom" needs to apply it here. The entire expression which now follows is wholly figurative, the number
seven and the mountains being symbolical. They symbolize the antichristian powers in all their plans and designs, and as strongholds which cannot be overthrown.
In these earth dwellers the purposes and designs of the
antichristian powers usurp the place that belongs to the
saving purposes of God (cf. 12:3; 13:1). The seven mountains, which are the seven heads of the beast, carry the
great whore, the antichristian seduction, so attractive to
the earth dwellers. Sitting upon the seven heads, or seven
mountains of the beast, this woman, exercising all the
power of the beast in her antichristian seduction, draws
the earth dwellers into her service and worship. The next
sentence, "and they are seven kings," properly belongs to
this verse, though placed in v. 10 in the Authorized Version. This sentence is also figurative, symbolizing the
thoughts, plans, and designs that usurp God's holy and
saving purposes.

V. 10 tells us that of these seven kings five are no
longer in action. They have already, previous to John's
time, succumbed to defeat in the years before Christ, and
have fallen. The description now advances to the two
head kings, or mountain kings, that are left. The first of

these here mentioned was active in John's time, and still continues in his activity, advancing the purposes and plans of the beast; but he also is destined to the same doom as the other five. The other one, whose doom will also be the same, has not as yet put in his appearance. Of this last of the seven kings John tells us that, according to God's purpose and ordination, he must remain for a little while; after which he will go the way of doom with the rest. These seven head kings in the service of the beast, zealously seeking to undermine the saving purposes of God and the Lamb, will not succeed, but will meet with an ignominious end.

V. 11 follows with a repetition of what was said of the beast in v. 8. Here it is declared that this beast is, in relation to these seven head kings, an eighth. As the seven head kings were apparently insufficient for the accomplishment of the evil designs of the beast, he himself comes to their aid. The clause "and is of the seven" in the Authorized Version, should according to the Greek text read: "and is out of the seven," as otherwise it places the beast on a level with his vassal kings. Here the final consummation is reached, and the beast himself, the eighth, goes into perdition.

The seven heads having now been explained, v. 12 proceeds to explain the ten horns. Here the number ten is significant as the symbol of completion. These ten horns, like the seven horns, are declared to be kings, but with this difference, that the ten horn kings have received no kingdom as yet, but are given authority with the beast for a short time. The ten horn kings represent the sum total of antichristian power in its most brutal form, which with a show of royalty exercises dominion and rule in company with the beast. These ten horn kings are represented as exercising authority for a brief period described as "one hour"; but they will rally to the support of the beast shortly before the end comes.

V. 13 describes the ten horn kings as having "one mind," i. e., one intent and purpose. In this they are all united. This one policy on which they are all absolutely agreed is to bestow all their power and authority on the beast for his use in the great and final battle that is to follow (cf. 16:13-14).

The outcome of this battle is described in v. 14. When at the beginning of this verse it is said: "These shall battle with the Lamb," the reference is to "the battle of the great day of God, the Almighty," for which battle the last of the seven head kings is preserved by God (v. 10) and receives power one hour with the beast (v. 12). The outcome of this battle is now set forth, viz., the complete subjugation and overthrow of the seventh head king together with the ten horn kings and all their hosts. The reason assigned for this overwhelming victory of the Lamb is that He is "Lord of Lords and King of Kings." These are not secular lords and kings, but are the Lamb's loyal vassals, his believing people, who according to 1:6 are made "kings and priests" unto God (cf. 1 Peter 2:9). The same appellation is given to Christ in the fuller description in 19:16. These followers of the Lamb are not mentioned here as aiding Him in conquering, but as being associated with Him and sharing in His royal victory. They are further described as "called," i. e., by the Holy Ghost through the Gospel; as "chosen," i. e., as elected from all eternity; and as "faithful," i. e., as those who have been preserved in the faith unto the end (cf. 1:5; 2:13; 3:14).

V. 15 explains what is meant by the expression "many waters." These are explained to be not literal waters, but "peoples and multitudes and nations and tongues." This enumeration is comprehensive and corresponds closely to

that given in 13:7. The seductiveness of the great whore
covers the whole world and allures and entices the earth
dwellers of all countries, races, classes, and conditions.

In v. 16 a great change of attitude on the part of
the beast and the ten horn kings is exhibited. In v. 7
the beast is shown carrying the whore; and in v. 13 the
ten horn kings are shown giving their authority to the
beast. Here they are represented as hating, stripping, devouring, and burning the whore. This change, as the next
verse shows, is brought about by God; yet it is also a
natural change. The whore, or antichristian seducation,
wins the earth dwellers for the beast, the antichristian
power, and so pleases the kings, or antichristian forces,
for a time; but eventually they realize the awful battle
that the whore is bringing upon them; and in their dis-
appointment they turn in furious rage against her. She
has not only lost all attraction for them, but has incurred
their bitterest hatred. The first act instigated by their
hate is that they forsake her, leaving her desolate, and
strip her of all her royal apparel and gorgeous jewels,
leaving her naked. The second act is that they devour
all her flesh, eating it voraciously as wild beasts devour
their victims. The final stage consists in their burning up
in fire this whore, described in v. 4 as serving in a golden
cup the abominations and unclean things of her whoring.
There is nothing remarkable about this. Antichristian seduction may delight for a while; but sooner or later it is
bound to prove disappointing. Then the rage of the victims knows no bounds. God overrules all things and
causes the antichristian forces to bring just retribution
upon one another. God frequently punishes sin with sin.

In the next verse the reason for the action just described is given. This reason is nothing else than the will
of God, who so rules and governs all things as to bring
them into His service for the accomplishment of His pur-

poses. God it is who put it into the hearts of the ten horn kings and of the beast to destroy the whore and to permit those who had hardened their hearts to follow the beast blindly and to give their kingdom to him. But, as the last clause shows, a limit is set to their activity beyond which they cannot go. When all God's prophetic words shall have reached their fulfillment, then the beast himself shall, like the whore, meet his destruction and final doom; but until this goal is reached, the beast will continue to exert his evil influence in the world.

In the last verse of this chapter it is explained that the woman is Babylon, i. e., the great antichristian empire as a whole, and specifically, the whole antichristian seduction (cf. v. 5). This woman, or Babylon, is here represented as exercising kingship over the kings of the earth. Her doom has been set forth in the preceding verses. The doom of the two beasts, the whole antichristian world power and the whole antichristian world propaganda, finds description in 19:19-21; and the doom of the dragon in 20:7-10. As a matter of fact, these three appear together and meet their doom together; but the doom of each is set forth in distinct and separate visions.

Chapter 18

1. *And after these things I saw another angel come down from heaven having great power; and the earth was lightened with his glory. 2. And he cried mightily with a strong voice, saying: Babylon the Great is fallen, is fallen, and is become the habitation of devils and the hold of every foul spirit and a cage of every unclean and hateful bird. 3. For all nations have drunk of the wine of the wrath of her fornication, and the kings of the earth have committed fornication with her, and the merchants of the earth are waxed rich*

through the abundance of her delicacies. 4. And I heard another voice from heaven saying: Come out of her, My people, that ye be not partakers of her sins and that ye receive not of her plagues. 5. For her sins have reached unto heaven, and God hath remembered her iniquities. 6. Reward her even as she rewarded you, and double unto her double according to her works; in the cup which she hath filled, fill to her double. 7. How much she hath glorified herself, and lived deliciously, so much torment and sorrow give her; for she saith in her heart: I sit a queen and am no widow and shall see no sorrow. 8. Therefore shall her plagues come in one day, death and mourning and famine; and she shall be utterly burned with fire; for strong is the Lord God, who judgeth her. 9. And the kings of the earth, who have committed fornication and lived deliciously with her, shall bewail her and lament for her when they shall see the smoke of her burning, 10. standing afar off for the fear of her torment, saying: Alas, alas, that great city Babylon, that mighty city! For in one hour is thy judgment come. 11. And the merchants of the earth shall weep and mourn over her; for no man buyeth their merchandise any more; 12. the merchandise of gold, and silver, and precious stones, and of pearls, and fine linen, and purple, and silk, and scarlet, and all thyine wood, and all manner vessels of ivory, and all manner vessels of most precious wood, and of brass, and iron, and marble, 13. and cinnamon, and odors, and ointments, and frankincense, and wine, and oil, and fine flour, and wheat, and beasts, and sheep, and horses, and chariots, and slaves, and souls of men. 14. And the fruits that thy soul lusted after are departed from thee, and all things which were dainty and goodly are departed from thee, and thou shalt find them no more at all. 15. The merchants of these things which were made rich by her shall stand afar off for the fear of her torment, weeping and wailing, 16. and saying: Alas, alas, that great city, that was clothed in fine linen and purple and scarlet, and decked with gold and precious stones and pearls! 17. For in one hour so great riches is come to naught. And every shipmaster and all the company in ships and sailors, and as many as trade by sea, stood afar off, 18. and cried when they saw the smoke of her burning, saying: What city is like unto this great city? 19. And they cast dust on their heads and cried, weeping and wailing, saying: Alas, alas, that great city, wherein were made rich all that had ships in the sea by reason of her costliness! For in one hour is she made desolate. 20. Rejoice over her, thou heaven and ye holy apostles and prophets; for God hath avenged you on her. 21. *And a mighty angel took up a stone like a great millstone and cast it into the sea, saying: Thus with violence shall that great city Babylon be thrown down and shall be found no more at all.* 22. *And the voice of harpers and musicians and of pipers and trumpeters shall be heard no more at all in thee; and no craftsman, of whatsoever craft he be, shall be found any more in thee; and the sound of a millstone shall be heard no more at all in thee;* 23. *and the light of a candle shall shine no more at all in thee; and the voice of the bridegroom and of the bride shall be heard no more at all in thee; for thy merchants were the great men of the earth; for by thy sorceries were all nations deceived.* 24. *And in her was found the blood of prophets and of saints and of all that were slain upon the earth.*

⸀he title of this chapter might well be: The Magnificence of the Great Whore and the Lamentation over Her.

The words "After these things," with which the first verse begins do not refer to an interval either small or great, but to the revelation made to John in Chapter 17. The angel in this vision is seen coming down out of heaven to appear above the earth, where Babylon lies in complete and final ruin. The description of this angel as "having great authority" is intended to emphasize the authoritative nature of his utterance. This is followed by a description of the effect of his appearance upon the earth. In the light of his heavenly glory the fate of Babylon is authoritatively and fully revealed.

In the second verse this angel is depicted as crying with a strong voice. The reason for this description of the voice is that it has so overwhelming a message of destruction to proclaim. The essence of this message is the absolute, irretrievable fall of Babylon the Great, made all the more emphatic here by the repetition of the word "fallen." The consequences of its fall are graphically

depicted in its having become "a habitation of demons
and a hold of every unclean spirit and a hold of every unclean and hated bird." For similar imagery in the Old
Testament compare Is. 13:21-22; 34:13-15. The scene pictured here is the horrible foulness and gruesome desolation of this city, once so great and so renowned, after
God's judgment has been poured out upon it.

Justification for the ruin that has befallen Babylon is
brought out in the third verse. Here it is shown that her
punishment, severe though it is, is nevertheless just, "because from the wine of the passion of her whoring all the
nations have fallen" (cf. 17:2; 14:8). Further justification
for the fate that has befallen her is afforded by the fact
that she has drawn to herself all the kings of the earth
and made them her paramours. A third point in justification of her punishment is the fact that the merchants of
the earth grew rich from the power of her wantonness.
These merchants are not literal merchants. The word
stands for all those who yield to antichristian seduction
and further its interests in all departments of human activity and life. These merchants are active in displaying
her wares and in selling her seductive goods, through
which they themselves become rich, not indeed in money,
but in that which is counted profit in Babylon the Great.
This completes the first section of this chapter.

The second section includes vv. 4-19. In v. 4 John declares that he heard another voice out of heaven, i. e.,
a voice that speaks from God (cf. 16:1). This is a voice
of warning with its message: "Come forth out of her, My
people." In the preceding verses Babylon's fall is described as having already occurred. Here Babylon is
viewed as still standing and offering enticements to par-
ticipate in her seductions. The words of this voice addressed to God's people are a call to them to come out of

Babylon and separate themselves from her and from all
for which she stands. The purpose of this warning, as the
words that follow show, is to save them from being over-
taken in Babylon's judgment (cf. Jer. 50:8; 51:6, 45; Is.
48:20; 52:11; 2 Cor. 6:17). It is a constant requirement
of God in His Word that His people whose fellowship is
with the Father and with His Son Jesus Christ, come out
from all situations and associations that would involve
them in the antichristian seduction for which Babylon
stands. All the seven plagues described in Chapter 16
will be visited upon all those who make common cause
with Babylon. Hence this emphatic call of God to His
people to come out of her that they receive not of her
plagues.

In v. 5 the reason for this demand is stated. It is because the sins of this wicked city form so great a mass
that they reach up to heaven itself and demand punishment at God's hands. To this it is added that God remembered her unrighteous acts. God's long-suffering is over,
and He remembers Babylon to execute upon her His just
retribution for all her unrighteousnesses (cf. 16:19). God
indeed bears long with the wicked; but His day of reckon-
ing will eventually come, and that with awfulness beyond
human description.

In v. 6 an injunction is given in reference to the judgment that is to be visited upon Babylon. By whom this
is done is not stated. With reference to this various conjectures have been made. The most probable solution is
that it is the angels of God, who as His ministering
servants execute His judgments, that give this injunction.
In the words "Render to her even as she rendered" strict
justice is enjoined. Babylon is to receive punishment in
exact accordance with what she meted out to her victims.
The words that follow, "and double to her double accord-

ing to her works," have been frequently misunderstood to
mean that she is to receive double punishment for her
evil deeds; but this would be a reflection upon God's
inexorable justice. In her works of seduction, Babylon
dealt out lavishly, i. e., dealt out "the double." It is only
just that she should receive the same doubling according
to her works. This is likewise brought out again in the
words pertaining to the cup. Just as she herself mixed
double whoring, so is the punishment to be mixed for her.
(Cf. the frequent references to the cup of the seductress
and to the cup of God's wrath, 14:8; 17:3; 14:10; 16:19;
17:2.)

V. 7 again enjoins that strict justice be meted out to
her according to the measure of her wantonness resulting
in torment and mourning. The reason for this is because
she is in a flourishing state, sitting and ruling as a queen,
exercising her seductive power without let or hindrance,
and being surrounded by a multitude of paramours, glory-
ing that she is not a widow. This condition she expects
will continue; and so she adds: "and I shall not see
mourning."

In v. 8 is described the result of Babylon's boasting
just recorded. Because of this her plagues will come in
one day, i. e., suddenly and unexpectedly; and that with
the most destructive power, described in such weird
terms as "death and mourning and famine," graphically
picturing the collapse of the whole antichristian seduction with all who are involved in it. All the earth dwellers
(cf. 13:16) will fall with the fall of Babylon. Her being
burned up with fire climaxes her complete destruction
and corresponds closely with what is said of her in 17:16.
By whom she will be burned up in fire is not stated here.
In 17:16 this is ascribed to the ten horn kings and the
beast. This does not, however, exclude their later mourn-

ing for her described later on. The last clause in this verse
explains why such overwhelming destruction has over-
taken her. It is none other than the judgment of the Lord
God that is now being executed upon her. He is here
designated "strong," His mighty strength being exhibited
in the doom visited on this great city of seduction.

The effect is sharply delineated in v. 9, where "the
kings of the earth," those that committed whoring with
her and lived wantonly with her, are pictured as mourning
for her in the most violent way. These kings, as the
paramours of the whore, symbolize the antichristian
powers that reign in the lives of the earth dwellers who
have succumbed to her antichristian seduction. The time
of their wild weeping and wailing is indicated in the
words: "when they see the smoke of her burning."

V. 10 dramatizes the lamentation made by these kings
over the fallen city. Literally translated, the opening
words read: "Woe, woe! The city! The great one, Babylon, the city, the strong one!" The word "strong" here
applied to Babylon is the same word that has just been
applied to God in v. 8, thus indicating Babylon as God's
competitor claiming for herself His prerogatives. God's
act of judging, though long delayed, came upon her suddenly and with such overwhelming destruction as to call
forth the weeping and wailing of the kings of the earth,
the merchants of the earth, and every shipmaster, and of
all those who had drunk of the wine of her whoring and
had lived luxuriously and wantonly with her.

This is described still more vividly and in greater detail in vv. 11-14. The merchants of the earth, here mentioned as weeping and mourning, include all in every
phase of human life and activity who sell any of the things
that pertain to antichristian seduction. The reason for
their excessive grief is that no one buys their cargoes
any more.

In vv. 12-13 a comprehensive enumeration of their cargoes is given, these verses mentioning things that are deemed most precious in this world and ending with human beings sold like animals, i. e., as slaves. This inclusive enumeration leaves no cargo of wares out of consideration. With the complete destruction of Babylon all these cargoes are without a buyer. Hence the excessive mourning of the merchants.

V. 14 depicts the effect upon the whore. The autumnal fruit, which she so much desired and lusted after, has departed from her forever; and the heyday of her lustful life has passed away nevermore to return. The desolation of the whore is complete. It not only affects her person, but also everything that pertains to her. None of the things in which she formerly delighted can be found in her any more (cf. Is. 3:16-24).

Further description of the merchants mentioned in the preceding verses now follows in v. 15. Their whole interest lies in the wares of the whore, the antichristian seductress, by whom they were made rich. Therefore it is said of them that they shall stand afar off for fear of her torment and, like the kings of v. 9, give vent to their emotions, "weeping and mourning."

V. 16 informs us of what these merchants say. Their utterance is quite similar to the utterance of the kings as given in v. 10; only here we have mercantile terms, descriptive of the clothing and adornment of the whore — adornment supplied by these merchants in order to increase her seductiveness.

In v. 17 the reason for their grief finds expression. It is because so great riches have so suddenly disappeared and can no longer be found in her. Next are described the seamen, including the captain of the ship who directs its course, the sailors in general, and all others who do work of any kind in the sea. All these, like the kings and the merchants, also stood afar off for fear of her torment.

In the succeeding verse these seamen are represented as giving expression to their feelings in words that disclose the depth of their grief, saying: "What city is like the great city?" In their eyes this city's greatness was incomparable. Their uncontrollable grief is expressed in the verse that now follows. The poignancy of their grief is manifested in their casting dust on their heads, in their loud crying accompanied by weeping and mourning, and in the words of woe which their grief calls forth (cf. v. 16). Why this great city was held in so high esteem by those who spend their lives and make their living on the sea was because of the expensive things in which she indulged and which she purchased from them. The cause occasioning their great grief is that all their trade is gone.

V. 20 introduces the third part of this vision, the heavenly side, which continues to the end of the chapter. Here God speaks, addressing heaven and calling upon its inhabitants to rejoice. Heaven's inhabitants, as far as humanity is concerned, are the saints, the Apostles, and the Prophets. Angels are not excluded from also participating in this joyful celebration. It is not, however, their victory that is celebrated, but the victory of the saints, the believers, over the antichristian seduction of the whore. The Apostles and the Prophets are the New Testament Apostles and the Old Testament Prophets, who, in their day and by their writings ever since, have been leaders in opposing antichristian seduction. The reason for the rejoicing of the heavenly inhabitants is because God has already executed His judgment upon Babylon, which resulted, as far as they are concerned, in the burning up of Babylon, or the complete destruction of the whore, or antichristian seduction. This judgment God exacted not on her, but from her.

In v. 21 is described the action of the angel in connection with the destruction of Babylon, together with its significance. This angel is called "strong" because of the action involved. It was a great stone like a millstone that he took up and threw into the sea. His action is symbolic, similar to that of Agabus (Acts 21:11) and to that of Jeremiah (Jer. 51:63-64). The words of the angel that follow describe the significance of his hurling of the big millstone into the sea. It signifies the violence by which Babylon should be thrown down to its utter destruction, so that the great city should not be found at all any more.

In v. 22 Babylon's total destruction is illustrated in three distinct statements: first, all sound of musical instruments is silenced; second, no craftsman of any craft is found any more; third, no millstone grinds flour any more.

The succeeding verse continues the illustration with two further statements. Fourth, no lamp lights up the darkness of night any more; fifth, no bridegroom or bride is heard any more. In the remaining words of this verse, answer is given to the question as to why such utter destruction has befallen Babylon. This was for two reasons: first, because her merchants were the grandees of the earth, pandering to the antichristian seduction by trading in its goods over the whole world; second, because with her sorcery all the nations of the earth were deceived. This deceiving is the work of the second beast (13:14) and of the dragon (12:9) and is a sin that properly calls down God's righteous vengeance.

V. 24 sets forth the climax of Babylon's overwhelming guilt. In her was found the blood of prophets, of saints, and of all martyrs. Her guilt was as great as her punishment.

Chapter 19

1. And after these things I heard a great voice of much people in heaven, saying:Alleluia! Salvation and glory and honor and power unto the Lord our God! 2. For true and righteous are His judgments; for He hath judged the great whore, which did corrupt the earth with her fornication, and hath avenged the blood of His servants at her hand. 3. And again they said, Alleluia! And her smoke rose up forever and ever. 4. And the four and twenty elders and the four living ones fell down and worshiped God, that sat on the throne, saying: Amen, Alleluia! 5. And a voice came out of the throne, saying: Praise our God, all ye His servants, and ye that fear Him, both small and great. 6. And I heard as it were the voice of a great multitude and as the voice of many waters and as the voice of mighty thunderings, saying: Alleluia; for the Lord God omnipotent reigneth. 7. Let us be glad and rejoice and give honor to Him; for the marriage of the Lamb is come, and His wife hath made herself ready. 8. And to her was granted that she should be arrayed in fine linen, clean and white: for the fine linen is the righteousness of saints. 9. And he saith unto me: Write: Blessed are they which are called unto the marriage supper of the Lamb. And he saith unto me: These are the true sayings of God. 10. And I fell at his feet to worship him. And he said unto me: See thou do it not: I am thy fellow servant, and of thy brethren that have the testimony of Jesus; worship God; for the testimony of Jesus is the spirit of prophecy. 11. And I saw heaven opened, and, behold, a white horse; and He that sat upon him was called Faithful and True, and in righteousness He doth judge and make war. 12. His eyes were as a flame of fire, and on His head were many crowns; and He had a name written that no man knew but He Himself. 13. And He was clothed with a vesture dipped in blood; and His name is called The Word of God. 14. And the armies which were in heaven followed Him upon white horses, clothed in fine linen, white and clean. 15. And out of His mouth goeth a sharp sword, that with it He should smite the nations; and He shall rule them with a rod of iron; and He treadeth the winepress of the fierceness and wrath of Almighty God. 16. And He hath on His vesture and on His thigh a name written: KING OF KINGS AND LORD OF LORDS. 17. And I saw an angel standing in the sun; and he cried

with a loud voice, saying to all the fowls that fly in the midst of heaven: Come and gather yourselves together unto the supper of the great God; 18. that ye may eat the flesh of kings and the flesh of captains and the flesh of mighty men and the flesh of horses, and of them that sit on them, and the flesh of all men, both free and bond, both small and great. 19. And I saw the beast and the kings of the earth and their armies gathered together to make war against Him that sat on the horse, and against His army. 20. And the beast was taken, and with him the false prophet that wrought miracles before him, with which he deceived them that had received the mark of the beast, and them that worshiped his image. These both were cast alive into a lake of fire burning with brimstone. 21. And the remnant were slain with the sword of Him that sat upon the horse, which sword proceeded out of His mouth; and all the fowls were filled with their flesh.

The first section of this chapter, vv. 1-10, presents the concluding portion of the vision begun in 17:1.

The opening words of v. 1, "After these things," refer to the things related in the last two preceding chapters. Here again John declares that he heard a great voice. This great voice is that of an immense multitude in heaven celebrating the fall of the great whore under God's judgment. This multitude is the same that John saw in 7:9 and, here as there, constitutes the one holy Church of all the saved. The utterance of this voice of the holy Church takes the form of an exclamation, ascribing to God the salvation which He has so graciously bestowed upon them, the glory which He thereby manifested, and finally the power exerted by Him in bringing about Babylon's fall.

The reason for the praise thus addressed to God is given in v. 2. First, just as in 16:7, God's judgings are declared to be genuine, i. e., without pretense or sham; and righteous, as meting out judgments corresponding to the

transgressions committed. Then God is also praised for
having exacted vengeance from the hand of the whore
who corrupted the earth for the blood of His saints which
she had shed.

In v. 3 these saints are presented as shouting "Hallelujah" a second time, ascribing praise to God for what
He has done, and as expressing the climax of God's vengeance upon the whore in the significant words: "And the
smoke of her torment goeth up forever and ever."

In v. 4 account is given of the impression made upon
the 24 elders, symbolizing the ministry of the Word, and
upon the four living ones, symbolizing the earthly agents
of God's providence, upon His wreaking of vengeance on
the whore. The account here is very similar to that of
the Throne Vision in 4:1-6. Both of these, here as there,
are closely connected with the throne, symbolizing God's
authority, rule, and dominion. In this verse the 24 elders
and the four living ones are represented as falling down
before the throne and worshiping God, thus joining the
vast multitude (v. 1) in celebrating the vengeance visited
by God upon the great whore, whose antichristian seduction has corrupted the whole earth. The sitting upon the
throne here ascribed to God implies that He is actively
exercising His power, rule, and dominion. These representatives of God's Word and agents of God's providence
confirm the hallelujahs of praise made by the vast multitude (vv. 1-3) with their "Amen," adding as a climax their
own "Hallelujah" to Him who sitteth upon the throne and
exercises His power, rule, and dominion therefrom. Thus
this vision is displayed in all its grandeur.

In v. 5 John tells us of a voice that came forth from
the throne. Whose voice this was, is not stated. It cannot
be the voice of God or the voice of the Lamb, neither of
whom could speak of "our God" (John 20:17); but as
coming from the throne, it is authoritative. This voice is

represented as addressing the whole vast multitude of the one holy Church consisting of all the saved. The call of this voice coming out from the throne is an exhortation to all the servants of God without exception to "praise our God."

In v. 6 John tells us that he heard "the voice of an immense multitude" (cf. v. 1). So great was the volume of this voice that he likens it to "the voice of many waters," such as cataracts and raging waves of the sea, and to the voice of strong thunders with their mighty reverberations. The message of this voice is "Hallelujah" (the fourth hallelujah in this vision), which means here as everywhere else: "Praise Jehovah." The reason for the ascription of Hallelujah to God is now stated. It is not, as our versions have it, because God *reigneth*, but because, viewing past history as a whole, God *reigned*. His plans have been carried out; His purposes have been accomplished; His will has been done. He is the Lord our God, the Almighty, whose plans never fail (Psalm 2; Psalm 110).

In v. 7 there is presented a call to rejoicing and exultation. This follows logically upon the last words of the preceding verse, "because the Lord our God, the Almighty, did reign." Why we should rejoice, exult, and give the glory to Him is stated in the words: "because the wedding of the Lamb is come and His wife did make herself ready." This brings us up to the wedding celebration which will take place in the second coming of Christ; but it does not depict or describe it. The time of the wedding has arrived. The bride of the Lamb, the holy Christian Church, the Church of true believers, has been made ready. This is the limit of the vision.

V. 8 now follows, showing that the readiness of the bride was not of her own doing, but that it was given to her, viz., by the grace of God thus to array herself for the wedding. Her garments are the best fine linen, shining

and pure. This fine linen, it is explained, is the righteousness, literally, the righteous acts of the saints. These
righteous acts are identical with the works that follow
those who die in the Lord (14:13). While the robe of
righteousness with which every believer is clothed is the
imputed righteousness of Christ, yet at the same time, by
virtue of their faith, which is ever active, they have also
the pure robes of their own righteous doings, which are
an evidence of the reality of their faith and of their being
clothed with Christ's perfect righteousness (cf. Matt.
25:34 ff.; 5:14; Eph. 5:27; John 13:10). This robe of
righteous acts, no less than the robe of Christ's righteousness, has been given to the saints and is a work of
God's grace in them.

In v. 9 John informs us that he received a command
from the voice that came from the throne (v. 5). The
command given was: "Write." What he was to write is
the great beatitude that follows. This beatitude is pronounced not only on those who at the end finally sit down
at the marriage supper of the Lamb, but it is pronounced
upon us and upon all who throughout all the centuries
have been called through the Gospel to the wedding supper of the Lamb in the Kingdom of Glory. Men may indeed turn down this call and exclude themselves from its
blessedness; but the call is addressed to them nevertheless. God is not willing that any should perish, but would
have all men come to the knowledge of the truth and be
saved. As confirming the beatitude just given the speaker
asserts, as John writes down what he saw and heard in
the vision, that these are the genuine words of God. For
this real call of God we should be truly grateful.

V. 10 records John's response to this great beatitude.
To the question: Why did he fall down to worship this
speaker? the only answer is, that he mistook the speaker
for the Lord Himself. To the further question: Why did

he, then, record it? the only answer is, that the Lord, whose revelation this is, so willed it. The speaker sternly forbids John's worship of him, declaring to him that he is John's "fellow servant" and "of his brethren that have the testimony of Jesus." These words of the speaker are a strong testimony that he is not an angel, but one of the saints in glory. This is in full accord with his calling God "our God" (v. 5) and with his calling upon the holy Church to praise God (cf. 3:21). The speaker's positive command, "Worship God," which immediately follows, is in full agreement with the Lord's own words in Matt. 4:10. In his concluding words the speaker explains the testimony of Jesus as "the spirit of prophecy," i. e., the inner content of all divine prophecy. The reference is to the Word of God, the everlasting Gospel of our salvation. Those who hold to the testimony of Jesus will worship God and Him alone.

Beginning at v. 11 and continuing to the end of the chapter, we have a description of the battle between the Lord and the beast. John saw here heaven opened for the Lord and His armies to go forth. In the word "behold" John calls attention to what he saw here as something of more than ordinary importance. It was a white horse and One sitting upon him. This One described as "faithful and genuine" is none other than the Lord Jesus Christ Himself, who comes as King of Kings and is followed by the armies of heaven (cf. 3:14). By "faithful" is meant that He to whom it is applied is absolutely trustworthy; and by "genuine," that there is no sham whatever about Him. The present tenses of the verbs in the last clause of this verse indicate timelessness. The Lord comes in righteousness to judge and to do battle with the beast unto his destruction. The judging here is literal; the doing battle, symbolical. Both describe the last great act of Christ the King. The complete vision of this final judgment is given in Chapter 20.

Vivid description of Jesus Christ as the Supreme Warrior is given in v. 12 and continued in the verses that follow. In describing His eyes as "a flame of fire" we have a repetition of what was said in 1:14. This expression describes His eyes as all-penetrating and as burning up His enemies. The further description of Him as having many diadems on His head, diadems being symbols of royalty, indicates that all royalty is His. In regard to the description of Him as having "a name written which no one knows but Himself," all conjecture is useless.

In v. 13 the description continues. The picture presented here shows Him as wearing a robe bathed in blood. The reference in this is to the blood of expiation shed by Christ, "the Lamb of God, which taketh away the sin of the world." It should be noted here that it is not the blood of His enemies, but His own blood, with which His robe is bathed. The words that follow, "and His name has been called the Word of God," imply that this has been given to Him to designate Him as being in His Person the final saving revelation of God. John is the only New Testament writer who uses this name (cf. John 1:1-3, 13-14; 1 John 1:1-2).

A description of His armies now follows in v. 14. These armies following the Lord as His attendants are here characterized as heavenly armies, which according to the analogy of the Holy Scriptures are composed of the holy angels (cf. Matt. 24:31; Luke 9:26). As riding upon white horses, they are marked as coming in holiness. This is further emphasized by the description of them as clothed in fine linen, white and pure. The holy armies of heaven accompany the Lord on His punitive expedition for the final destruction of the beast.

V. 15 describes Christ in action in this great battle.

The first thing here noted is a sword, a sharp one, proceeding out of His mouth to accomplish its destructive
work on the nations, the earth dwellers, who are the
enemies of God and of the Lamb. The second clause
indicates that the time for Him to smite the nations with
a rod of iron (cf. Ps. 2:9) has now arrived and that their
complete destruction is at hand. The third clause discloses the actual execution of God's wrath by Christ Himself (cf. 14:19-20). This is a fulfillment of Is. 63:1-3 and
is depicted in the most intensifying terms. Just as the
grapes were trodden (14:20), so now are God's enemies
crushed.

In v. 16 the Lamb is further described as having the
name "King of Kings and Lord of Lords" written on His
robe and on His thigh, where it could be readily seen
and easily read. The kings and lords here mentioned are
not the kings of the earth, but the Lamb's loyal followers,
who as believers have been made kings and priests to
God and the Lamb.

In v. 17 John tells of a single angel that he saw standing in the sun, and reports his message. This angel stands
in the sun, the heaven being opened that the King with
His army may ride to battle. With a loud voice this angel
called to all the birds that fly in midheaven, such as the
vultures, eagles, and other carrion eaters, to come to the
great supper which God has provided for them and to
feast upon the carrion so abundantly prepared. Similar
summonses are found in the Old Testament (Deut. 28:26;
Jer. 7:33; 16:4; Ezek. 39:17-20); but this one surpasses
them all.

In v. 18 is set forth the purpose of the angel's summons, and incidentally the results of the battle in the multitudinous corpses of all classes that fell in it. The purpose
here was that these carrion eaters might satiate themselves in devouring the victims of this immense slaughter.

The whole antichristian power has now reached its end, and all the antichristian forces have come to ultimate destruction in the last judgment, which is symbolized by this last battle.

In v. 19 John states in detail what he saw in this vision, viz., the beast, the kings of the earth, and their armies — all these gathered together for battle against the King and His army (cf. 19:11-16; 13:1-8). The beast symbolizes the whole antichristian power; the kings of the earth, the antichristian forces; and their armies, all the lesser forces under their management and control. These are all personifications; but they also involve human persons. The dragon, who is back of all these, is a personal being, and is none other than Satan himself.

The result of the battle is told in vv. 20 and 21. It resulted first of all in the capture of the beast. This was followed by the capture of the false prophet, who so faithfully supported him and wrought signs whereby he deceived those that had the mark of the beast and those that worshiped his image (13:11-18; 16:15). The final fate of the beast and the false prophet is now stated as the casting them alive into the lake of fire and brimstone. As the beast and the false prophet are not actual beings, but personifications, the meaning is that they are absolutely overpowered and destroyed, their adherents and followers being actually cast into hell (cf. 14:10).

In the last verse of this chapter, account is given of the fate of all who constitute the forces or armies of the beast. Here it is stated that they were killed, not by the armies of the King, but by the great sword that proceeded out of His mouth (cf. v. 15; 1:16; 2 Thess. 2:8). The obedience of the birds to the summons given them is recorded in the words: "and all the birds were gorged with their flesh." The final fate of these wicked armies is recorded in 20:15.

Chapter 20

1. *And I saw an angel come down from heaven having the key of the bottomless pit and a great chain in his hand. 2. And he laid hold on the dragon, that old serpent, which is the devil and Satan, and bound him a thousand years 3. and cast him into the bottomless pit and shut him up and set a seal upon him, that he should deceive the nations no more till the thousand years should be fulfilled; and after that he must be loosed a little season. 4. And I saw thrones, and they sat upon them, and judgment was given unto them. And I saw the souls of them that were beheaded for the witness of Jesus and for the Word of God, and which had not worshiped the beast, neither his image, neither had received his mark upon their foreheads or in their hands; and they lived and reigned with Christ a thousand years. 5. But the rest of the dead lived not again until the thousand years were finished. This is the first resurrection. 6. Blessed and holy is he that hath part in the first resurrection; on such the second death hath no power, but they shall be priests of God and of Christ and shall reign with Him a thousand years. 7. And when the thousand years are expired, Satan shall be loosed out of his prison 8. and shall go out to deceive the nations which are in the four quarters of the earth, Gog and Magog, to gather them together to battle; the number of whom is as the sand of the sea. 9. And they went up on the breadth of the earth and compassed the camp of the saints about and the beloved city. And fire came down from God out of heaven and devoured them. 10. And the devil that deceived them was cast into the lake of fire and brimstone, where the beast and the false prophet are, and shall be tormented day and night forever and ever. 11. And I saw a great white throne, and Him that sat on it, from whose face the earth and the heaven fled away; and there was found no place for them. 12. And I saw the dead, small and great, stand before God; and the books were opened: and another book was opened, which is the Book of Life; and the dead were judged out of those things which were written in the books, according to their works. 13. And the sea gave up the dead which were in it; and death and hell delivered up the dead which were in them; and they were judged every man according to their works. 14. And*

death and hell were cast into the lake of fire. This is the second death. 15. And whosoever was not found written in the Book of Life was cast into the lake of fire.

A good title for this chapter would be: The Thousand Years and the First Resurrection. The term "thousand years" occurs six times in vv. 2-7 of this chapter. It covers the whole period treated from 12:1 to 20:6, or from the appearance of the dragon (12:3) to his final judgment (20:7-10), the same names being assigned to him in 20:2 as in 12:9. The thousand years actually cover the whole New Testament dispensation from the incarnation and enthronement of the Son of God (12:5) to the final casting of Satan into hell (20:10). This chapter is divided into four sections. The first section, vv. 1-3, shows the state of the dragon during the New Testament dispensation. The second section, vv. 4-6, exhibits the state of the martyrs, who, remaining steadfast in their faith unto death, did not receive the mark of the beast or worship him (20:4) The third section, vv. 7-10, portrays the final doom of the dragon. The fourth section, vv. 11-15, presents the vision of the Judgment.

In the first verse John tells us that he saw an angel coming down out of heaven. Just who this angel was, we are not told. In view of Christ's words in 1:18: "I have the keys of death and of Hades," some have conjectured that this is a designation of Christ, who as God's Messenger is represented here as descending out of heaven for His incarnation. But two facts are against such interpretation. One is that the term "angel" is never in Revelation applied to Christ; and the second is that in 9:1 the key to the abyss was given to the angel there mentioned. The angel, here as there, exercises not his own authority, but the authority of Christ, whose ministering servant he is. The abyss of which this angel holds the key is none other than hell, "the lake of fire burning with brimstone" (19:20). There is only one such place in the other world known to the Scriptures, and that is hell. This angel is further pictured as carrying a great chain in his hand for the binding of Satan. But these terms are not to be understood literally. The key symbolizes the power to open and close hell; and the chain, the power to render Satan helpless.

The second verse pictures this angel in action. His first act was to seize and overpower the dragon, here, as in 12:9, designated as "the devil and Satan." His second act immediately following the first was the binding of Satan. The duration of this bondage is definitely stated as "a thousand years." This "thousand years," a round number, is not to be taken literally, but symbolically in accord with the imagery with which it is surrounded. It stands here for the present dispensation, or the period of the Messianic reign (cf. Heb. 2:14-15; 1 John 3:8) till near its close, when Satan shall be loosed again for a little time (v. 3), and shall go forth to deceive the nations that are in the four corners of the earth (v. 7). It is with this thousand years' bondage of Satan that the Chiliasts start spinning out their millenarian theories. Taking the thousand years as a literal number, they maintain that during this period Satan is absolutely bound; that all his agents, such as the beasts and the whore, are banished; that Christ and His saints during this period reign peaceably and without interruption upon the earth; and that the Jews will be converted, and everything will be lovely as long as the thousand years last; but that at the end of this period this admirable state will come to a sudden close, and evil will again become rampant and gain the ascendancy. All such views are properly characterized in the Augsburg Confession as "certain Jewish opinions" and are there condemned. As a matter of fact, the thousand years in this chapter of Revelation begin with the binding and imprisonment of Satan, or in other words, with the advent of Christianity, when Satan's power was curbed, so that he could no longer deceive the nations with the success that was his previous to the proclamation of the glorious Gospel of human salvation. The Millenarians who place the thousand years in the past are unable to point to any period in past history that even remotely corresponds to the description given in these verses. And those among them who place the thousand years in the future are found to depart sharply from the analogy of the Scriptures and of Christian faith. In contradiction to the clear teaching of Scripture they abolish all ideas of a general resurrection and divide the resurrection into two parts separated by a thousand years, placing the resurrection of the just before and the resurrection of the unjust after the thousand-year reign of Christ and His saints. Over against such views cf. Christ's own words in John 5:28-29 and Matt. 25:31 ff. Then to complete the picture which they formed in their own imagination they lug in Old Testament passages which have no bearing whatever on the Millennium, such as, e. g., Is. 11:6-9; 65:25.

The description of the action of the angel in relation to the dragon, i. e., the devil, or Satan, is continued in v. 3. The angel, after having bound the dragon, cast him into the abyss, i. e., into hell, and locked and sealed it over him. Thus there was no possibility for him to escape as long as the thousand years lasted. This binding of Satan is frequently referred to in the Scriptures (cf. Gen. 3:15; John 16:11; Col. 2:15; Heb. 2:14; 1 John 3:8; Rev. 12:7ff.). The locking and the sealing symbolize the certainty and the completeness of the dragon's confinement and its continuance during the thousand years. The purpose of this was that Satan might no longer work directly, as he formerly did, in his nefarious work of deceiving the nations. This also explains why in the two preceding visions (that of the two beasts and that of the whore) Satan himself does not appear, but works through his agents. This binding of Satan means that he cannot prevent the heralding of the Gospel throughout the world for a testimony to all nations. He can no longer work directly. There remains only the antichristian propaganda (19:20) to seduce the nations; and this can deceive only those who, like the kings and their armies, are willing to be deceived. Satan, the mighty foe, has been stopped from his direct and immediate work. Only the two beasts and the whore are now working; and this will be the case during the thousand years, or the complete New Testament dispensation. The last clause of this verse tells us that at the end of the time when the Gospel is preached, i. e., after it has accomplished its work in the world, Satan must be released. This release, however, is only for a brief period, i. e., just long enough for him to gather his hosts together that the fire out of heaven might devour them (v. 9). A description of the final work of Satan is given in vv. 7-8 (cf. Matt. 24:12; 21:24; Luke 18:8). The work of the Gospel having been accomplished, the final judgment of Satan follows shortly thereafter.

In v. 4 John tells in a vividly descriptive way of the thrones that he saw and of the souls of the martyrs living and reigning with Christ during this "thousand years." Thrones, as we have frequently seen before, symbolize power, rule, authority, and dominion; and "sitting upon thrones," the putting to exercise of such rule. We note here that it was souls that John saw. The contention of some, that these souls must have had bodies or John could not have seen them, is perverse rationalism. But this is characteristic of the millenarians, who pervert not only the term "souls," but also "the first resurrection" in order to make these fit into their theory. Souls here, as in 6:9, are spoken of as being bodiless. To interpret 2 Cor. 5:1 as meaning that souls are given bodies in the other world immediately after death is a serious misinterpretation. It is definitely stated here that these martyrs endured unto death for the sake of the testimony of Jesus and the Word of God, i. e., on account of their faith. John further informs us here that he saw another group of those occupying the thrones, consisting of all those that worshiped not the beast or his image and received not the mark on their forehead and on their hand. The implication here is that he saw the souls of all the departed saints, or all the souls saved during the present dispensation. The whole purpose of this vision is to reveal the royal exaltation and power of every martyr and faithful believer, when at his death his soul enters into heaven.

In v. 5 John tells us of the condition of the rest of the dead, i. e., of those who did not live and reign with Christ. Concerning all these, who died in unbelief, he declares that they did not live. (The word "again" in our Authorized Version should be omitted, it not being found in the original manuscripts.) As was the case with the martyrs, the souls of these unbelievers also left their bodies on earth. Their souls, however, did not live, but continued their existence in a state of spiritual death with all that it involves. This was their situation throughout the thousand years. The distinction drawn between them is quite clear. During this period the godly die as to their bodies, but their souls live on in a blessed heavenly life. During the same period the ungodly also die a bodily death, but their souls, far from living and reigning with Christ, continue to exist in a state of spiritual death with all the misery that it entails. This state continues throughout the thousand years. Immediately upon this will follow the resurrection of all souls, i. e., the reuniting of all souls with their bodies. Then, in body and soul, the godly will partake of the life which their souls lived in heaven during the thousand years. The bodies of the ungodly will likewise be raised and reunited with their souls, but without the life which these souls never had during the New Testament dispensation of grace; and in body and soul they will partake of that death which is eternal. In the last words of this verse where John says: "This is the first resurrection," there can be no doubt that the reference is to what he has just said in v. 4 of the souls of the martyrs and of the saints living and reigning with Christ in eternal glory. Accordingly, the resurrection of which John here speaks is a resurrection pertaining to souls. The term is not used here in a literal, but in a symbolic sense, signifying a quickening and raising up as in Eph. 2:6. Additional proof is that the Scriptures know of only one bodily resurrection, viz., the general resurrection of both the godly and the ungodly at the Last Day.

In the next verse a beatitude is pronounced upon each and every participant in this first resurrection. This blessedness brings happiness in the highest degree to him on whom it is pronounced. He is further declared to be "holy." This implies the removal from the soul at death of every trace of sin as it rises up into heaven to sit upon its royal throne. Every soul thus rising has part in the "first resurrection" and is blessed and holy. This is the positive reason for the beatitude. The negative reason is that the second death has no authority over any of the partakers of the first resurrection and cannot possibly touch them, because as priests of God and of Christ they shall reign with Him a thousand years. We are here reminded of the promises made by God to believers (1:6; 5:10; 1 Pet. 2:9) — promises pertaining to their present life. But here they are described as priests of God and of Christ in the perfection of holiness in heaven. In the final clause the

"thousand years" must not be understood as setting a
limitation to their reigning; but the expression is a natural
one in view of what follows in the next verse, which
speaks of what will happen after the thousand years are
finished.

In vv. 7-8 there is set forth another view of the last
battle, previously presented in 16:12 ff. and in 19:11 ff.
The special feature here is that everything is focused
upon Satan. In Chapter 12 Satan appears as the dragon,
and as such as the instigator of all antichristianity. Thereafter, however, he disappears, because he has been bound.
Nevertheless he continues his operations through the first
beast, the antichristian power, and through the second
beast, the antichristian propaganda. These in their turn
produce Babylon, the whore, symbolizing the antichristian seduction. All these have been previously described
as having reached their end, which will come at the close
of the thousand years, or the end of the New Testament
era after the Gospel shall have completed its work among
the nations (Matt. 24:14). When this goal has at last
been reached and the whole number of God's saints have
been brought into the fold, then the end will come. Then
Satan shall be loosed out of his prison and shall go forth
to deceive the nations in the four corners of the earth,
his deception reaching its climax in the gathering together
of the nations for the battle, the great battle, the Armageddon (16:13 ff.).

V. 8 pictures Satan in action carrying out his last deception. This consists in gathering the nations from the
four corners of the earth for the last great battle. He per-
suades these nations to believe that with one concerted
action they will be able to overthrow Christianity and an-
nihilate it from the earth forever. All this takes place in
the "little while" of v. 3. In describing the nations that
Satan deceives as "those that are in the four corners of the

earth," they are pictured as including the whole earth and embracing all the earth dwellers. These nations are further defined as "Gog and Magog" cf. Ezek. 38:2; 39:6). Gog is the name of the prince and leader; and Magog, the name of his land and people. Both these dreadful enemies of Israel were annihilated by a rain of fire, hail, and brimstone on the mountains of Israel. Just as it was with them, so will it be with the nations in the four corners of the earth, the Gog and Magog, in the last great battle with Almighty God. Gog and Magog stand as representatives of all opposition to Christianity and the Christian Church, such as New Theology, New Thought, Mormonism, Russellism, Christian Science, and other radical sects; and also materialism, carnalism, sensualism, birth control, and all other forces of sin that seek to corrupt the Church and kill her inner spiritual life. In this great battle all these will meet their final doom. In likening the number of warriors composing this Satanic host to the "sand of the sea," there is an indication of the vastness of the multitude gathered by Satan for the last great battle against Almighty God.

V. 9 gives an account of the battle and its outcome. So great were the hordes of Satan that they covered the whole expanse of the earth as they gathered themselves together for this last decisive battle. They are pictured here as encircling the camp of the saints and the beloved city. The situation of the saints, of their camp, and of their city seems desperate, notwithstanding the fact that this city is described as "the beloved city," i. e., the city that is the object of God's love. But God intervenes to save His saints, their camp, and their city from the destruction aimed at them by Satan and his hordes. God sent forth fire out of heaven, which devoured them. Thus were their shrewdly laid plans for overpowering the saints put to confusion; and the hordes of Satan perished in utter destruction (cf. Ezek. 38:22). The devil and his forces may indeed plan to destroy God's kingdom and His people; but "He that sitteth in the heavens shall laugh; the Lord shall have them in derision" (Ps. 2:4; cf. Prov. 1:26).

In v. 10 the doom of the devil himself is depicted. We are not left in any doubt as to what became of him, but are expressly told that he was cast into the lake of fire and brimstone, where already his agents, the beast and the false prophet, had preceded him (19:20). He is described here as the one that deceived them, this being his distinctive characteristic from the beginning (v. 3). Now that the limit of his reign of deception has been reached, he is consigned to the lake of fire and brimstone, where together with his agents and his followers he endures never-ending torments. From the terrible torture of this endless, unremitting torment there is not a moment's relief or alleviation, as the words "by day and by night" clearly testify.

From v. 11 to the end of the chapter we have a description of the Judgment. This is presented for the most part in literal language, and exhibits the final fate of all antichristianity and antichristian power and seduction. The throne here is no ordinary throne, but a "great white throne" — the supreme throne, the throne from which the Final Judgment of the universe proceeds. This throne, here as elsewhere, symbolizes power, rule, and dominion. That it is white symbolizes that the judgments proceeding from it are holy judgments. John, however, saw not only the throne itself, but also Him that was sitting upon it. From Matt. 24:30; 25:31 we conclude that this was none other than the Son of Man, Christ Himself, to whom all judgment was committed by the Father (cf. 19:1, 11, 16). The reference here, as the words that immediately follow show, is to no preliminary judgment, but to the great and final Judgment at the end of the world. From before the face of this great Judge both the earth and the heaven, on and under which Satan had built up the kingdom of darkness, fled as unable to endure the flaming eyes of this Judge; and to make the picture more intense, it is added: "and no place was found for them." This does not necessarily imply the annihilation of the heaven and the earth, but rather a renovation or rejuvenation of them (cf. 21: 1-5; Rom. 8:22; *et al.*).

The description of this judgment vision continues in v. 12. In John's assertion that he saw the dead, all are included who underwent physical death from Adam on to the end of the world. The comprehensiveness of this term is emphasized by the addition "the great and the small," thus indicating that not a single one who has died will be missing from among those standing before the throne. This corresponds with the analogy of Scripture in reference to the general Judgment (cf. Matt. 25:31-33; John 5: 28-29; Rom. 14:10; 2 Cor. 5:10). All these passages are a clear refutation of the chiliastic conception of a double resurrection, one at the beginning and the other at the close of the so-called Millennium. The next clause in this verse deals with the opening of the books pertaining to Judgment. What these books contain may be seen from the Lord's picture of the general Judgment in Matt. 25:31 ff. These books contain the records of the guilt and condemnation of the unbelieving and ungodly according to their deeds. The other book opened is the Book of Life (cf. 3:5), in which are written the names of all true believers, who were faithful unto death (13:8). Open books, we note, are Old Testament symbols of judgment (cf. Ex. 32:32-33; Dan. 7:10). Two features characterizing the judgment are that men were judged from the things written in the books and that they were judged according to their works. This is the consistent teaching of Scripture and is repeated and individualized in v. 13. These books are not to be understood as being literal books. They are figurative representations of the infallibility of the omniscient Judge, before whom all things are naked and open. These books contain the record of all the dead, the bad and the good; but they contain no record of the bad works of the saved, since these have been blotted out of the book of God's remembrance, "nailed to the cross and taken out of the way," all their sins having been washed away in the blood of the Lamb. Their good works serve in the Judgment as public evidence of the faith of the believers. And so believers also are judged according to their works.

V. 13 furnishes complete proof that all dead bodies will be raised. While the sea only is mentioned as "giving them," this is not to be taken exclusively. Since a body sunk in the depths of the sea is recovered, there is no question regarding bodies in the earth. It makes no difference where men have died, whether on land or sea, or in lakes or rivers, their bodies will be reunited with their souls and will come forth at the resurrection. And it makes no difference whether the souls of these dead were in heaven or in Hades, they must be reunited with their bodies and appear before the judgment seat of Christ, where they will be judged, each one according to his works. This means that the Lord will render sentence according to their faith, or their unbelief, manifested in their works. And from this sentence there will be no appeal to all eternity. Death, as separating the soul from the body, includes all, both believers and unbelievers alike. Hades, as the abode of the souls of the unbelieving, contains only the souls of the damned. The judgment sentence will be pronounced publicly on both the godly and the ungodly (cf. Matt. 25:34, 41).

Vv. 14-15 set forth the inevitable result that follows in this judgment vision. In a figurative way it is indicated here that the end of death, which came into the world as the result of sin, and the end of Hades is the same as that of Satan himself, viz., to be thrown into the lake of fire (cf. 1 Cor. 15:26). These figurative expressions signify that death will be destroyed and that Hades will never again receive a wicked soul, but will henceforth be swallowed up in Gehenna, or the lake of fire, which is the second death, in which all the wicked are tormented eternally in both body and soul. This is hell in its fullest state (cf. Matt. 10:28). The last verse in this chapter describes the carrying out of the sentence pronounced by Christ the Judge as the final Judgment (cf. Matt. 25:46). Nothing is said here concerning the godly, or those whose names are written in the Book of Life. These come in for treatment in the last two chapters of Revelation.

Chapter 21

1. *And I saw a new heaven and a new earth; for the first heaven and the first earth were passed away; and there was no more sea.*
2. *And I, John, saw the Holy City, New Jerusalem, coming down from God out of heaven, prepared as a bride adorned for her husband.* 3. *And I heard a great voice out of heaven saying: Behold, the tabernacle of God is with men, and He will dwell with them, and they shall be His people, and God Himself shall be with them and be their God.* 4. *And God shall wipe away all tears from their eyes; and there shall be no more death, neither sorrow, nor crying, neither shall there be any more pain; for the former things are passed away.* 5. *And He that sat upon the throne said: Behold, I make all things new. And He said unto me: Write; for these words are true and faithful.* 6. *And He said unto me: It is done. I am Alpha and Omega, the Beginning and the End. I will give unto him that is athirst of the fountain of the water of life freely.* 7. *He that overcometh shall inherit all things; and I will be his God, and he shall be My son.* 8. *But the fearful and unbelieving and the abominable and murderers and whoremongers and sorcerers and idolaters and all liars shall have their part in the lake which*

burneth with fire and brimstone; which is the second death. 9. And there came unto me one of the seven angels which had the seven vials full of the seven last plagues, and talked with me, saying: Come hither, I will show thee the bride, the Lamb's wife. 10. And he carried me away in the spirit to a great and high mountain and showed me that great city, the holy Jerusalem, descending out of heaven from God, 11. having the glory of God; and her light was like unto a stone most precious, even like a jasper stone, clear as crystal; 12. and had a wall great and high, and had twelve gates, and at the gates twelve angels, and names written thereon, which are the names of the twelve tribes of the children of Israel: 13. on the east three gates, on the north three gates, on the south three gates, and on the west three gates. 14. And the wall of the city had twelve foundations and in them the names of the twelve Apostles of the Lamb. 15. And he that talked with me had a golden reed to measure the city and the gates thereof and the wall thereof. 16. And the city lieth foursquare, and the length is as large as the breath. And he measured the city with the reed, twelve thousand furlongs. The length and the breadth and the height of it are equal. 17. And he measured the wall thereof, an hundred and forty and four cubits, according to the measure of a man, that is, of the angel. 18. And the building of the wall of it was of jasper; and the city was pure gold, like unto clear glass. 19. And the foundations of the wall of the city were garnished with all manner of precious stones. The first foundation was jasper; the second, sapphire; the third, a chalcedony; the fourth, an emerald; 20. the fifth, sardonyx; the sixth, sardius; the seventh, chrysolyte; the eighth, beryl; the ninth, a topaz; the tenth, a chrysoprasus; the eleventh, a jacinth; the twelfth, an amethyst. 21. And the twelve gates were twelve pearls; every several gate was of one pearl; and the street of the city was pure gold, as it were transparent glass. 22. And I saw no temple therein; for the Lord God Almighty and the Lamb are the temple of it. 23. And the city had no need of the sun neither of the moon to shine in it; for the glory of God did lighten it, and the Lamb is the light thereof. 24. And the nations of them which are saved shall walk in the light of it; and the kings of the earth do bring their glory and honor into it. 25. And the gates of it shall not be shut at all by day; for there shall be no night there. 26. And they shall bring the glory and honor of the nations into it. 27. And there shall in no wise enter into it anything that defileth, neither whatsoever worketh abomination or maketh a lie, but they which are written in the Lamb's Book of Life.

ᘔhe first eight verses of this chapter treat of the
New Heaven and the New Earth. The remain-
ing verses to, and including, the fifth verse of the succeeding chapter deal with the Bride of the Lamb.

In the first verse, in evident allusion to what he had
said in 20:11, John tells what took the place of the first
heaven and the first earth, which, fleeing from the face of
Him that sat upon the throne, had passed away, viz.,
"a new heaven and a new earth" (cf. Is. 65:17; 66:22; Matt.
24:29; 2 Pet. 3:10, 13). This does not imply an immediate
creation by God, but a transformation of the heaven and
the earth corresponding to that which takes place in the
bodies of believers at their resurrection, thus rendering
the heaven and the earth a fitting habitation for the saints
in light (cf. Rom. 8:20-23; 2 Cor. 5:17; Gal. 6:15; Eph.
2:10; 4:24). The last statement in this verse, "and the
sea is no more," is to be understood literally. In the new
heaven and the new earth the functions of the sea will no
longer be needed; hence it is not included in the new
creation.

The second verse describes the Holy City, New Jerusalem, descending out of heaven from God. The beauty
of the New Jerusalem is here appropriately described in
the words: "prepared as a bride adorned for her husband." God's presence (v. 3) makes this city holy; and
as a city it is filled with God's people who have been made
ready as the bride of Christ and adorned with His gifts.

In the next verse John tells of a voice which he heard
and its gracious message. Whose voice this is we are not
told; but as coming out of the throne, it speaks about God
and for Him; and because of the exceeding importance
of its message this voice is described as "a great voice."
The great message of this voice is that the tabernacle of
God is with human beings, implying that God Himself
shall dwell with them, and they shall be His people, and

God Himself shall be with them. This is a presentation of the final consummation of all God's plans and purposes with reference to human beings. The meaning here is that with all human beings, except those consigned with the devil and his angels to the lake of fire and brimstone, God Himself shall dwell; that there will be no more separations or divisions among them, but the closest union and communion between them and God — a holy fellowship which God Himself initiates and continues to all eternity.

V. 4 furnishes an enumeration of blessings that flow from this holy fellowship. The first of these is that God will wipe away every tear from their eyes. In striking contrast to conditions as they exist in this present evil world, where countless tears are shed, there will henceforth be nothing to call forth tears. God's constant presence and blessing will be sufficient to dry all tears from every eye. The second of these blessings is that for the godly now in their eternal state of glory death has been altogether abolished through Jesus Christ, and with it all issuing therefrom, such as mourning, crying, and pain, which are the cause of so many tears in this present world. The reason assigned for this is that the former things have passed away and are no more. The great and glorious fact here stated is that the saved are in a happy state from which evil and all its consequences are absolutely excluded.

In the fifth verse Christ Himself, designated as "He that sitteth on the throne," is presented as speaking. Sitting upon the throne and exercising all authority in heaven and in earth, He declares: "Behold, I make all things new." In this life by the grace of God so richly bestowed upon us, we believing Christians are made new creatures in Christ Jesus. This will reach its consummation when He will make all things new. From Christ sit-

ting upon His royal throne there comes a command to
John to write down what has been said in vv. 3-4 together
with what follows in vv. 6-8. And the reason assigned for
this order is that these words are true and faithful, i. e.,
free from all deception and fraud, and trustworthy and
reliable. This expression is of frequent occurrence in this
book (cf. 3:7, 14; 6:10; 15:3; 16:7; 19:2, 9).

V. 6 furnishes proof for the faithfulness and genuineness of the words above referred to. What these words
say are realities that have already occurred. Christ has
already made all things new. This John simply sees and
here records. Christ here proclaims Himself to be "the
Alpha and the Omega, the Beginning and the End" (cf.
1:8, 17). He is Alpha and Omega as God's full and complete revelation from the first to the last letter. As "the
First and the Last" He is all history from start to finish.
As "the Beginning and the End" He is God's saving work
from its inception to its consummation (Lenski). To this
description of Himself Christ now adds for the comfort of
the believer who, having drunk of His grace, now thirsts
for His glory, an exceedingly precious promise, assuring
him that He will give him of the water of life freely, thus
fulfilling to him the promise already made in 7:17 to lead
him to life's springs of waters. This thought receives still
fuller development in 22:1, 17.

In v. 7 Christ gives a second promise to the believer
here described as the conquering one — a promise of an
exceedingly encouraging nature, assuring him of victory
in the contest in which he is engaged. This promise is
that he shall inherit all the new things on the new earth;
and, to make this assurance doubly sure, He adds that He
will be his God and that he shall be His son.

In v. 8 Christ continues His discourse with a word of
warning — a warning which we Christians should ever
bear in mind and take to heart. Here various classes are

mentioned who have no faith and hence no part in Christ,
but whose portion is in the lake that burneth with fire
and brimstone. The cowards are those who, overcome by
fright, give up the good fight of faith and so fail to conquer. The unbelievers are those who have proved unfaithful. Those who have become abomination are such
as have raised immoral stench by their lives and actions.
The murderers, whores, and sorcerers are designations of
various types of spiritual abominations (cf. 17:5-6; 18:23).
Idolaters are those who worship false gods. All liars are
such as follow the second beast, the false prophet or the
lying one (16:13; 19:20; 20:10). All these shall have their
part in the lake that burns with fire and brimstone, which
is the second death (cf. 20:14; 22:15). There is absolutely
no support here for the chiliastic notion of a thousand
years' reign of Christ and His saints on earth. There is
also just as little reason for picking out Old Testament
passages which describe the new earth in colors taken
from the peace of Paradise as applying to the Millennium,
as, e. g., Is. 2:4; 65:25.

V. 9 begins the description of the bride of the Lamb,
the Holy City, Jerusalem. The angel appearing here is
in all probability the same angel that appears in 17:1, the
introduction being identical in each case. The message
delivered is, however, quite different. In 17:1 it centers
in the judgment of the great whore. Here it deals with
the bride, the wife of the Lamb, or the holy Christian
Church composed of all the glorified saints, picturing the
Church as it appears after the *parousia* (coming) of Christ
in its final state of glorification. Here the Church appears
in all her glorious bridal decorations, as again in 22:17.

John continues his description in v. 10. The opening
words in this verse correspond closely with those in 17:3.
The expression "in spirit" here, as in 1:10 and 4:2, refers
not to the Holy Spirit, but to John's own spirit. What

John saw here was "in spirit"; and so glorious was this
vision that in order to enable him to see it, the angel
carried him away in spirit into a great and high mountain.
The language here used is intended to convey something
of the greatness and glory of that which John was granted
to see not with natural, but with spiritual eyes. John has
already seen this vision (see v. 2); but this second vision
of the city coming down from God out of heaven reveals
to him much more than he saw in the first vision. The
high mountain from which he here views it enables him
to see the more clearly the wonderful sight of the Holy
City, Jerusalem, as it comes down from God out of heaven.
V. 11 states one of the new things revealed in this vision.
In vv. 1-8 it was the blessedness of God's union and communion with His people that was revealed. Here it is His
glory as it fills the Holy City – a marked advance over
the previous vision. The word "light" employed here in
our versions is more properly "lightbearer," or "luminary"
(cf. Phil. 2:15). Here this luminary causes the city to
shine with heavenly radiance. This figure of speech is
enhanced by the similes that follow. It is described as
being "like a most precious stone, as it were a jasper, clear
as crystal." A similar description is given in 4:3, where
two precious stones are mentioned. The probability is
that the stone there called "jasper" was not a jasper
(which is opaque and colored and not a precious stone),
but a diamond. This appears still more to be the case
here, where it is described as scintillating, or sparkling.
The other stone mentioned in 4:3 is here omitted because
the judgment which it symbolized is already past. The
"lightbearer" in this verse is undoubtedly God. This is
made clear from v. 23 and from the analogy in 4:3.

The description of this city continues in vv. 12-14. The
first feature noted is that it is a city with walls great and
high. Such walls in ancient Eastern cities were designed

for protection and constituted the chief defense against assault and siege; but this purpose cannot be attributed to the wall of this Holy City, since it is not to be conceived of as occupying any local space on earth. This great and high wall symbolizes inclusion in the eternal union with God. The twelve gates or portals signify entrance into the eternal union with God (cf. v. 26). At these portals were twelve angels, one at each portal (cf. Gen. 3:24). Here an angel is represented as standing at each portal to welcome those entering into this eternal union with God. We are further informed that the names inscribed on these portals are the names of the twelve tribes of the sons of Israel, God's chosen people. These represent the whole number of the saints in the Kingdom of Glory, the 144,000 mentioned in Chapter 7. They are mentioned again in the 24th verse of this chapter, where their blessings are further described. In 7:9 they are declared to be "a great multitude which no man can number" (cf. 7:16-17; 21:6). The portals and the angels here play an important part in making clear the significance of this eternal union with God.

V. 13 sets forth the distribution of the twelve portals on the wall of this symbolical city. On each of the four sides of the wall are three portals, symbolizing catholicity, i. e., universal prevalence or universal acceptance. This catholicity is perfect and complete on the new earth; and the prophecies of Isaiah, chap. 43:5-6, and of our Lord in Matt. 8:11 are perfectly fulfilled (cf. Matt. 28:19; Mark 16:15).

V. 14 concludes the description of the symbolical city, the New Jerusalem that came down from God out of heaven. The twelve foundations on which the walls of the city rest symbolize the writings of the Apostles in the New Testament, the inspired writings, on which the eternal union with God rests (cf. Eph. 2:20; Luke 21:33).

On the foundations of these walls, we are told, were the names of the twelve Apostles of the Lamb — those who had been commissioned by Him to preach His Word to all nations throughout all time. This they did, and still do through the New Testament Scriptures, through which Christ Himself speaks. It is quite true that not all the Apostles wrote in the New Testament Scriptures; yet those who did write by inspiration of God wrote for them all. Twelve is the number symbolical of the Apostles, just as it is of the tribes of Israel. There is no reason here for excluding St. Paul from this number, since in Chapter 7 twelve represents the tribes of Israel, although the tribe of Dan is left out of the enumeration.

In v. 15 the measuring of the Holy City is described. The speaker here is the angel mentioned in v. 9. It is stated here that this angel had as a measure a golden reed. In 11:1-2 we are told that John himself was given a reed to measure the holy Church on earth, and that he did this with his rod, which, however, was not golden. Here the rod is in the hand of the angel and is golden because of the glory of the city that came down from God out of heaven. The purpose of this rod in the angel's hand was that he might measure the city, its portals and its wall.

In the verses that follow, the dimensions of the city and its wall are given. While nothing is said about the dimensions of the portals, it may be explained that they are included in the measurement of the wall.

In v. 16 is set forth the first result of this measuring, viz., that the city forms a perfect square. It follows, therefore, that the length and the breadth are equal. The angel measured the length of the city, 12,000 stadia. The city being a perfect cube has all sides equal. No spatial relation is indicated by this number. The measurement of this Holy City, built not by man or by angel, but by God

Himself, is symbolical. The number 12 symbolizes the holy Church in its glorified condition in heaven. This raised by the multiple of 1,000, the number of utmost completeness and perfection, symbolizes God's union with the holy Church in the eternal perfection designed by God and consummated through the Lamb. This city here pictured was foreshadowed by the Holy of Holies in the Tabernacle and in Solomon's Temple, which were also perfect cubes. The cube with its three identical dimensions symbolizes perfection. Into the Holy of Holies of the Tabernacle no one save the High Priest could enter, and he only once a year. The Holy City, the New Jerusalem, of which this was a type, symbolizes the eternal union of God with all His people.

In v. 17 account is given of the measuring of the wall. This wall, also symbolical, is measured by the same 12 as to its length, height, and breadth. The wall denotes inclusion and is marked in all directions by 12, the number of God's people. Its length, height, and enclosed area, all in twelves, indicating inclusion, picture the eternal union of God with His people as symbolized in the Eternal City.

The next verse describes the material with which this city was built — material magnificent beyond all human imagination. First is described the building of the wall. The material, called "jasper" in our versions, was most probably diamond. The entire city was built of gold, the most precious of all metals. This gold, being of the purest quality, is described as "pure gold, like unto pure glass," which means that it glittered and shone with all the brilliancy of polished glass.

Vv. 19-20 describe the foundations and their adornment by the Builder with all kinds of precious stones. Twelve of these are now enumerated. A few of these stones are known and may be identified; but it is practically impossible to identify them all. The difference be-

tween these stones is without symbolical significance.
It is also impossible to identify them with the 12 stones
on the breastplate of the Jewish high priest. The symbolism here is comprehensive. As symbolizing the eternal
union with God resting upon the apostolic foundation of
the Gospel, these stones are the most precious that can be
imagined. They are not the small precious stones with
which we are familiar, but are of incomprehensible size
as representing the preciousness and the beauty of the
eternal basis of the union of God with His people.

In v. 21 a description of the portals follows. The
portals, as we have seen before, symbolize our entrance
into eternal union with God. That they are twelve, is
symbolical of the number of the covenant. So immense
are these pearls that each of these portals is made of a
single pearl. This figure is quite appropriate, reminding
us of "the pearly gates of heaven." The broad street or
avenue of the city to which all the portals open, here
likened to pure gold like transparent glass, is also magnificent beyond human description.

In v. 22 John comes forth with a negative statement,
telling us what he did not see in this city. He saw no
temple in it. He explains at once why this was so. It was
because the Lord God Almighty and the Lamb are this
city's temple. Consequently, there was no need of a
temple; the eternal union of God Almighty and the Lamb
with His people is immediate and complete, and all the
saved are in eternal communion with God. The whole
city is filled with God's glorious presence. This negative
statement is continued in v. 23. Besides the absence of
a temple, there was also the absence of the sun and the
moon from this Holy City; and the reason assigned for
this is that these luminaries were no longer needed because the glory of God illuminated it, and the Lamb is its
Lamp. By "the glory of God" is meant God Himself; and

by "the Lamb" is meant the incarnate Son of God, who
died for us. This glory fills the whole city with its un-
created light. The blessed state of the saved is brought
out in v. 24. The nations here mentioned as walking in
its light embrace all who dwell in this city — "a great
multitude," "out of every tribe and tongue and people and
nation," who are "made a kingdom and priests unto God"
(cf. 5:9; 7:9). These nations are not literal nations, but
stand for the whole multitude of the saved. "The kings
of the earth" here mentioned are not literal kings, but
symbolize those among the great and powerful on earth
who were not won over to the service of the dragon, but
became followers of the Lamb. Of them it is declared
that they shall bring their glory into the city. This, which
is repeated again in v. 26, gives symbolical expression to
what has already been stated literally in 14:13. What
these kings accomplished during their earthly career for
the Lamb follows them; and for this they receive a gracious reward in the Eternal City. The description continues in the remaining verses of this chapter.

In v. 25 it is emphatically stated that the portals of this
city shall not be shut. This shall not at all occur by day,
and cannot occur by night because there shall be no night
there. The reference in this whole description is to the
timeless moment indicated in v. 2 when the Holy City
comes down to the new earth. The statement "and they
shall bring the glory and honor of the nations into it,"
v. 26, corresponds to what is said of the kings in v. 24; and
the explanation given there holds good here. The good
works of all the saved accompany them and are acknowledged by God, who assigns to them His gracious reward.
This city, symbolizing the eternal union of God and of
the Lamb with all the saints, comprises the whole new
heaven and new earth, leaving no vacant spaces in them.

V. 27, the last verse in this chapter, stresses emphati-

cally the kind of people excluded from entrance when the
Lamb brings His own into this city. First of all are excluded all the unholy. No unholiness will or can be
tolerated in any of the Lord's saints. Then everyone that
worketh abomination or maketh a lie is excluded. Every
such one has his portion not in the Holy City, but "in the
lake that burneth with fire and brimstone." No one will
be found there "save those whose names are written in the
Book of Life of the Lamb" (cf. 20:12; 15:3, 5; 13:8).

Chapter 22

---

1. *And he showed me a pure river of water of life, clear as crystal,
proceeding out of the throne of God and of the Lamb. 2. In the
midst of the street of it and on either side of the river was there
the tree of life, which bare twelve manner of fruits, and yielded
her fruit every month; and the leaves of the tree were for the
healing of the nations. 3. And there shall be no more curse; but
the throne of God and of the Lamb shall be in it; and His servants
shall serve Him. 4. And they shall see His face; and His name
shall be in their foreheads. 5. And there shall be no night there;
and they need no candle, neither light of the sun; for the Lord God
giveth them light; and they shall reign forever and ever. 6. And
he said unto me: These sayings are faithful and true; and the Lord
God of the holy prophets sent His angel to show unto His servants
the things which must shortly be done. 7. Behold, I come quickly;
blessed is he that keepeth the sayings of the prophecy of this book.
8. And I, John, saw these things and heard them. And when I had
heard and seen, I fell down to worship before the feet of the angel
which showed me these things. 9. Then saith he unto me: See thou
do it not; for I am thy fellow servant and of thy brethren, the
prophets, and of them which keep the sayings of this book; worship
God. 10. And He saith unto me: Seal not the sayings of the
prophecy of this book; for the time is at hand. 11. He that is unjust, let him be unjust still; and he which is filthy, let him be filthy*

*still; and he that is righteous, let him be righteous still; and he that
is holy, let him be holy still. 12. And, behold, I come quickly; and
My reward is with Me, to give every man according as his work
shall be. 13. I am Alpha and Omega, the Beginning and the End,
the First and the Last. 14. Blessed are they that do His commandments, that they may have right to the tree of life and may enter
in through the gates into the city. 15. For without are dogs and
sorcerers and whoremongers and murderers and idolaters, and whosoever loveth and maketh a lie. 16. I, Jesus, have sent Mine angel
to testify unto you these things in the churches. I am the Root and
the Offspring of David, and the bright and Morning Star. 17. And
the Spirit and the bride say: Come. And let him that heareth say:
Come. And let him that is athirst come. And whosoever will, let
him take the water of life freely. 18. For I testify unto every man
that heareth the words of the prophecy of this book: If any man
shall add unto these things, God shall add unto him the plagues
that are written in this book: 19. and if any man shall take away
from the words of the book of this prophecy, God shall take away
his part out of the Book of Life and out of the Holy City and from
the things which are written in this book. 20. He which testifieth
these things saith: Surely I come quickly. Amen. Even so, come,
Lord Jesus. 21. The grace of our Lord Jesus Christ be with you all.*

---

*I*n the first section of this chapter, vv. 1-5, the
description of the Holy City, begun in the
preceding chapter, continues; and this is followed by a
delineation of the blessedness of life in the golden city
as revealed to John.

In v. 1 John declares that in this vision the angel
showed him a river of life's water, thus indicating its
exhaustless abundance. The description of this river of
life's water as "bright as crystal" implies that no impurity
whatever is associated with it, but that it reflects the
purity of absolute holiness. It is further pictured as proceeding out of the throne of God and of the Lamb. What
John is actually shown here is the whole stream of eternal
life proceeding from the throne, or eternal power, of God
and the Lamb.

V. 2 contains a description of the tree of life. The
translation of this verse in our Authorized Version is not
very clear and is still more inaccurate in the Revised
Version. It is better to take the expression "in the midst
of" in the sense of "between," i. e., in the middle, with the
avenue on one side and the river on the other. The ad-
verbs are added as indicating "from here" and "from
there," i. e., from the avenue looking across the river and
from the river looking across the avenue. In the space
between the avenue and the river stood the tree of life.
These terms, like those in 21:21, are to be understood collectively and include all the avenues, all the rivers, and
all the trees of life to be found in the city. The tree of
life means the tree which gives life, or more accurately
still, the tree which is life. Life in the eternal union with
God is symbolized by these rivers and by these trees to indicate its fullness and abundance. The term here used in
the original for tree is not the usual word for tree, but
the regular word for wood, reminding us of the cross,
which is the wood or tree of life (cf. Acts 5:30; 10:39;
13:29; Gal. 3:13; 1 Pet. 2:24). This tree is pictured as
bearing twelve fruits, 12 here as elsewhere being the
symbolical number referring to the holy Church. The
tree, as bearing its fruit each month, is represented as
rendering it perpetually without cessation. Human terms
are inadequate to describe the timelessness of eternity.
Similar symbolism is here applied to the leaves of this
tree, which are said to be for the healing of the nations,
i. e., the nations of the saved.

V. 3 sets forth negatively and positively the blessedness of the saved. Negatively, within this Holy City there
shall be no more any accursed thing, i. e., no person will
be admitted there who, having incurred the wrath of God
and come under His curse by a life of sin and unbelief,
would by his presence mar the perfect bliss of heaven.

Positively, the blessing for the inhabitants of this Holy
City consists in the throne of God that is in it, or God's
complete rule, dominion, and power. God actively exercising His authority, His servants willingly and gladly do
Him service constantly and unceasingly.

V. 4 presents the beatific vision of God which these
servants have in their glorified state. They look straight
into the face of the Lamb, whom they served in this life.
Their vision of Him is an immediate vision, no longer
mediated through the Word. Infinitely blessed and glorious will their service be as they gaze upon their Lord face
to face and see Him as He is. In the statement "His name
shall be in their foreheads" we are reminded of what was
said in 7:3 of the sealing of the servants of God on their
foreheads, which occurred when they were brought to
faith in Jesus Christ. Now as saved forever, they bear
Christ's name upon their foreheads — a symbol of God's
saving revelation, marking them as His own forever.

In v. 5 is described the serving of these saints in the
light of glory and their reigning eternally with their Lord
(cf. 21:23). In 1:6, near the beginning of this book, it is
stated that Christ made us to be a kingdom and priests to
His God and Father. Here, near its close, it is said of
His servants in the Kingdom of Glory that they shall reign
forever and ever. Christ reigning over them is confirmation of His title "King of Kings and Lord of Lords"
(19:16). This verse closes the first section of this chapter.

The second section (vv. 6-21) contains a record of
visions and their attestation. In these verses are set before
us God's attestation, Jesus' attestation, John's dismissal,
and his farewell greeting.

In v. 6 the angel is represented as addressing John
again. Although this angel is not named, it is beyond
doubt the same angel mentioned in 1:1, John deriving his
expressions in 1:1-3 from what the angel says here in this

and the following verse. The words at the beginning of this verse, "These words are faithful and genuine," refer to the whole Book of Revelation and are an attestation of it by this angel whom God employed to show these visions to John. Since God uses this angel in making His revelations, the testimony of the angel, who is God's representative, is the testimony of God Himself. This, of course, applies not only to this angel, but also to all angels whom God commissions to bring His revelations to men. In the closing words of this verse the Lord, who is here designated as "the God of the spirits of the prophets," is declared to have commissioned His angel to show to His servants the things that must shortly occur. In the designation of God given above it is implied that God inspired the prophet's words in opening his mouth to speak and in taking his pen in hand to write. The revelation here communicated to John, this angel is to show first to John, and then through him to all God's servants, viz., to all believing Christians.

In v. 7 the angel quotes Christ, calling attention to the importance of His words by the expression "And behold." In the words, "I am coming" we are reminded of the title "the Coming One," which Jesus applies to Himself in 1:8, a title applied to God in 1:4 and 4:8. The word "quickly," which the Lord applies to His coming, does not designate the time of the *parousia* as coming soon after these visions were given. Jesus does not come only at the *parousia*, but comes in all the innumerable judgments occurring throughout the succeeding centuries that point to the final Judgment as their consummation. The beatitude that now follows is a repetition of the beatitude in 1:3. It is pronounced by the angel upon him that keeps as a priceless treasure the words of the prophecy of this book. Just as the angel's attestation is God's attestation, so is his beatitude God's beatitude.

In v. 8 the impression made upon John by the things which he saw and heard in these visions is described. So overwhelming was this impression that John was moved to fall down and worship the being that showed these things to him. John had acted once before in the same way, mistaking his revealer for his Lord, and was reproved for his action (cf. 19:10). But now, upon hearing the words "Behold, I come quickly," he feels sure that he is in the presence of his gracious Lord, and at once falls before his feet in adoring worship. And, while the words that follow show that he was mistaken again, yet he was not mistaken in his expectation that Jesus would Himself appear and attest His revelation. This actually occurred (vv. 16-19). It should be noted, however, that it is not Jesus who here addresses John, but His angel.

The absolute prohibition of the worship of the angel by John is given in v. 9 in practically the same words used in 19:10, the only difference being that in the latter passage all Christians are included in one group, "those having the testimony of Jesus," while here they are divided into two groups, "the prophets and those keeping the words of this book." John in writing the words of this book is exercising a prophetical function; and the angel in aiding him in this work was his fellow servant and of his brethren, the Prophets. The testimony of this angel, who is God's representative, is God's own testimony.

In v. 10 an injunction is given to John by this angel. The injunction was that he was not to seal the words of the prophecy of this book, implying that he was to do the very opposite, viz., to publish them. The reason given is: "for the season is near." This statement, found in the beginning of this book and now repeated at its close, refers to the period in which the things recorded in this book will occur. Thus from beginning to end the words of this book are attested by God through His angel.

Further words of the angel follow in v. 11; and they
are words of great significance. The message here is:
If the unrighteous and the filthy will not be warned by
the words of the prophecy of this book, they will inevitably receive their due reward and reap what they have
sown. Likewise the righteous and the holy, made such by
God's grace, will receive their reward of grace.

In v. 12 we have again the angel speaking and quoting
the words of the Lord, as was the case in v. 7. Here, however, are added the words: "and My reward is with Me
to render to each one as his work is." This reward is the
Lord's own gracious reward and is given by Him to each
one in proportion to the work he has done in His service
from the active side of faith (cf. 20:12; Matt. 25:31-46).

The angel's quotation of the words of the Lord continues in v. 13. The words quoted furnish the Lord's
threefold attestation by ascribing to Himself attributes
comprehending God's revelation, all history, and all God's
saving work (cf. 1:8, 17; 2:6; 21:6).

V. 14 records a second beatitude (v. 7) and recalls
what was said of the 144,000 in 7:14. It is pronounced
upon those who wash their robes, i. e., in the blood of the
Lamb, or in other words, those who are His true and
faithful followers. In what their blessedness consists is
also pointed out. It is that they have right to the tree of
life and to enter by the portals into the Holy City.
(N. B. The Authorized Version's reading, "they that do
His commandments," is not only not well attested, but
disagrees with 7:14.)

V. 15 declares who shall not enter the Holy City: unbelievers, deliberate transgressors of God's Law, spiritual
adulterers, idolaters — all that lie and practice deceit.

From v. 16 to v. 19 inclusive we have the attestation
of the second Witness, who is none other than Jesus Christ
Himself, "the faithful and genuine Witness." Jesus says

here: "I sent My angel to testify these things in regard to the churches." "These things" are identical with "the things that must occur shortly" (v. 6). In calling this angel "My angel" Jesus does not refer to any special angel, but to whatever angel God and Jesus employ in making revelation in any vision. He calls Himself here by the name He received at His incarnation, "Jesus" — a name of the utmost significance. It is His name as the incarnate Son of God. This is the name most frequently used for Him in the Apocalypse. In addition to the titles which He ascribes to Himself in v. 13, He adds here: "I am the Root and the Offspring of David, the Brilliant, the Morning Star." In speaking of Himself as the Root of David, there is plainly a reference to Is. 11:1, "root" being used here in the sense of "shoot," which springs from it. "Offspring" is to be understood literally as applying to Christ according to His human nature. This is amply attested in the genealogical tables of Matthew 1 and Luke 3. In speaking of Himself as "the Brilliant, the Morning Star," His royalty is symbolized in the highest degree (cf. 2:28).

In v. 17 an exceedingly gracious invitation is extended in words spoken by the Lord Jesus Christ Himself. In the opening words, "And the Spirit and the bride say: Come," the Spirit is the Holy Spirit, and the bride is the Church, not indeed in heavenly glory, but as she appears on earth. During the present dispensation the Spirit and the bride unite in the one single invitation, "Come." This invitation is to be repeated by everyone who hears and heeds the invitation of the Spirit and the bride, the Church. Two exhortations now follow. The one is: "Let him that is athirst come," and the other: "Let him that willeth take life's water freely." These are earnest invitations to partake of the promise given in 21:6. To bring into such participation is the whole purpose of this book. Hence it is so strongly attested.

In v. 18 Jesus Himself still speaks. The substance of
His testimony here is that to anyone adding to the things
that are written in this book, God will add the plagues
that are written in it. This positive threat should be sufficient to deter anyone from such corruption of the text.
But as the words of the prophecy may also be corrupted
by the removal of words from it, the negative side is
presented in v. 19. The declaration here is that in case
anyone should take away from the words of the book of
this prophecy, God shall take away his part from the tree
of life and from the Holy City and from the things written
in this book. The consequences in each case are the same
and are in accord with strictest justice. It is God that
affixes the penalty in both cases: He would not be the
just God that He is if He could do otherwise. This testimony of Jesus concerning the sacredness and importance
of this book applies strictly only to the Book of Revelation; but His testimony to this last prophetic book of the
New Testament should analogically move us to hold as
sacred and unalterable the truth and doctrine found in all
the books of the New Testament as constituting the
Gospel, which testifies of Jesus Christ, the one and only
Savior from sin.

V. 20 records the conclusion of the testimony of Jesus
and the dismissal of John. His testimony is the same that
He has uttered before: "Yea, I come quickly." This John
confirms by answering: "Amen" and adding to it the
fervent prayer: "Come, Lord Jesus."

In the 21st verse, the last verse in this chapter, John
concludes his message and blesses his readers. In the beginning of this book, grace and peace were extended as
a greeting to the seven churches. Here at the close a
benediction of peace is bestowed upon them. This is
closed with an Amen of confirmation.